I0427690

TABLE OF CONTENTS

I. INTRODUCTION

The North Korean nuclear weapons issue has culminated in a climactic standoff between the ill-equipped and undernourished nation and the rest of the world. In the last year, Kim Jong Il, the reclusive leader of the Democratic People's Republic of Korea (DPRK) (commonly known throughout the world as North Korea), has continued to defy the world community regarding missile testing and the desire to possess nuclear weapons. Indeed, North Korea launched several missiles in July 2006 into the Sea of Japan, and in October 2006 conducted its first ever nuclear weapons test. According to multiple news outlets world-wide, the regime could conduct yet another nuclear weapons test, and North Korean government officials indicated testing of a nuclear missile "depends on how the U.S. will act."[1] With North Korea becoming a confirmed nuclear power, the potential for radical instability in the Northeast Asian region exists to a greater degree than ever seen before in the post-Cold War era. The challenge for the United States and the world community is exactly how to handle this possibly disastrous turn of events.

Since the January 2002 State of the Union speech in which President Bush declared North Korea to be part of an "Axis of Evil," the Bush Administration has attempted a diplomatic solution to this conflict. To confront the growing unease on the Korean Peninsula and at the urging of Washington, Beijing established talks between North Korea, the United States, and China, and then later invited South Korea, Japan and Russia to keep the United States engaged.[2] The addition of the these three countries placated Washington since the Bush Administration maintains that the most rational

---

[1] "U.S. Vows Not to Be Intimidated by North Korean Threats" (Fox News, accessed 23 October 2006); available from http://www.foxnews.com/story/0,2933,219121,00.html; Internet.

[2] John S. Park, "Inside Multilateralism: The Six-Party Talks," *The Washington Quarterly,* Vol. 28 no. 4 (Autumn 2005): 76.

means to end the nuclear standoff on the Korean Peninsula is for North Korea to negotiate with all of the regional governments most affected by the DPRK weapons program. These Six-Party Talks began in August 2003, with the first meetings held in Beijing. A second and then a third round of talks were held in February and June 2004, culminating in a fourth round of talks in September 2005. Upon completion of this session, North Korea "committed to abandoning all nuclear weapons and existing nuclear programs and returning, at an early date, to the Treaty on the Non-Proliferation of Nuclear Weapons and to IAEA safeguards."[3] However, after this seemingly positive step, subsequent meetings were delayed for over a year by North Korea, and a crisis erupted with Pyongyang's nuclear detonation. North Korea expressed its desire for one-on-one discussions with the United States, but the United States resisted such talks despite indications that the Six-Party talks' members would be open to a bilateral exchange between the two nations.[4] Following North Korea's nuclear test, the multilateral talks reconvened in December 2006 and again in February 2007. A tentative agreement between North Korea and the others regarding the DPRK nuclear weapons program was announced following the latest round of talks.

Prior to 2001, the Clinton Administration did conduct direct talks with North Korea. The result of negotiations conducted in Geneva between representatives of both governments was the 1994 Agreed Framework, which called for North Korea to refrain from producing fissile material from its declared nuclear facilities in exchange for energy related assistance from the United States and other allies. For a variety of reasons,

---

[3] U.S. State Department, *Joint Statement of the Fourth Round of the Six-Party Talks* (Washington D.C.: Bureau of Public Affairs, 19 September 2005, accessed 23 October 2006); available from http://www.state.gov/r/pa/prs/ps/2005/53490.htm; Internet.
[4] "Direct Talks Urged With N. Korea," *The Washington Times*, 23 October 2006.

including North Korean duplicity and the American political system, the Agreed Framework did not eliminate the nuclear issue on the Korean Peninsula. President Clinton attempted to reengage with the DPRK in 2000 by sending the Secretary of State to meet with Kim Jong Il directly. The meetings netted no additional agreements before the Clinton Administration departed office. Overall, the bilateral negotiations conducted with North Korea during the Clinton Administration did provide for substantial progress on the issue, but netted no permanent resolution.

The Bush Administration policy of preemption when required, and the aggressive nature of its rhetoric regarding rogue states, may have caused North Korea to believe it may be the next battlefield enemy for the United States military, and hence continue its missile and nuclear weapons testing. With the Global War on Terrorism and continued operations in Iraq, it is imperative that the United States avoid another military crisis – a crisis which the Department of Defense would be hard pressed to resource. A diplomatic solution must be seriously explored and would be in concert with American published strategic documents from the highest levels.

Beginning a line of bilateral negotiations with North Korea outside of the Six-Party Talks will allow the United States to meet its strategic goals related to the Global War on Terrorism that apply to the Korean peninsula, including the elimination of the North Korean nuclear threat. To support this thesis, this paper will explore the history of the DPRK, along with past and current United States policy towards North Korea. The paper will also explore the interests and policies of the nations involved in the Six Party Talks, investigating whether the nations involved can truly negotiate from one united viewpoint. Additionally, it will take a critical look at case studies of governments which decided to give up their nuclear weapons ambitions, specifically investigating the motivation for these governments and how the decision was reached in each individual case. It will examine whatever lessons can be learned from these events which the United States can use when working towards a resolution of the current conflict. Finally, this study will review United States strategic documents in an effort to define Washington's strategic interests on the Korean peninsula, and provide recommendations to accomplish successful bilateral negotiations with the hermetic regime of North Korea.

II. HISTORICAL POLITICS OF THE PENINSULA

A. The Korean Peninsula after World War II

To fully appreciate the situation on the Korean Peninsula, its history must be understood. A small measure of planning for a post-World War II Korea began during the Cairo Conference in 1943, where the United States, China, and Great Britain agreed that Korea would be an independent state free of Japanese occupation. At the Yalta Conference in February 1945, President Franklin D. Roosevelt proposed a tri-national trusteeship over Korea, with the United States, China, and the Soviet Union providing oversight. Marshal Joseph Stalin of the Soviet Union agreed with the concept, but no final decisions were made regarding Korean governance.[5]

In May 1945, Harry Hopkins visited Moscow to discuss bilateral relations between the two allied powers, and Korea was briefly discussed. It was here that the State Department hoped for agreements on Korean trusteeship, as the United States was concerned that Korean exiles living in the Soviet Union during the war would return and give Moscow instant influence. The United States was hoping to install local Koreans in governmental positions.[6] With opposing viewpoints concerning governance, no agreement was reached. During the Potsdam Conference, where the allied leaders discussed the post-war world, the future of Korea was only mentioned by low level staffers and military personnel. The leaders of the allied nations did not discuss the topic

---

[5] Library of Congress Federal Research Division, *South Korea Country Study* (Washington D.C.: Library of Congress, 2005, accessed 18 February 2007); available from http://lcweb2.loc.gov/cgi-bin/query/r?frd:@field(DOCID+kr0022); Internet.

[6] William Stueck, *Rethinking The Korean War* (Princeton: Princeton University Press, 2002), 21.

at all.[7] The lack of discussions and planning regarding the Korean Peninsula during the war would set conditions for a quick but not well thought out solution by allied powers as the war against Japan was coming to its climactic conclusion.

Dividing Korea at the 38th parallel was a political solution born in the offices of the Army Operations Division in Washington. Brigadier General George Lincoln, working with the State Department's James Dunn as members of the State-War-Navy Coordinating Committee (SWNCC), settled on that line as a proposal for dividing Korea between Soviet and United States troops as both nations planned for occupation of the peninsula. The Soviet Union had declared war on Japan in between the United States' atomic bomb attacks on the cities of Hiroshima and Nagasaki. Shortly after the war declaration, Soviet troops had invaded the northern portion of the Korean Peninsula. With Japan now making overtures concerning surrender, the State Department noted the Soviet invasion and wanted the Army to quickly invade the peninsula as well so that the country could be divided equally between the two nations' occupation forces when the war was over.

The 38th parallel division was subject to minimal scrutiny when planning the details of the Japanese surrender and made its way into the draft General Order Number One, put together for President Truman's review on 15 August 1945. President Truman approved it in short order, and the draft was then sent to Moscow for the Soviet Premier, Joseph Stalin, to review. With no further discussion among nations, Stalin agreed to the occupation line in Korea.[8]

---

[7] U.S. State Department, *Foreign Relations of the United States: Diplomatic Papers: The Conference of Berlin (The Potsdam Conference)* (Washington D.C.: U.S. Government Printing Office, 1945, accessed 17 February 2007); available from http://digital.library.wisc.edu/1711.dl/FRUS.FRUS1945Berlinv02; Internet.
[8] Stueck, 12.

The division of Korea provided the United States with a means to control Soviet influence in the region. There was no other reason for it, as the United States had little if any strategic interest in the peninsula itself. For its part, Moscow did have an historical interest in the region, as the pre-Soviet Russian Republic did fight a war with Japan over interests in Manchuria and Korea. However, the two major powers did not concern themselves at all with what the division did to the people of the peninsula, those who had suffered a brutal Japanese subjugation for more than a generation. As Bruce Cummings writes in his book, *Korea's Place in the Sun: A Modern History,*

> There was no historical justification for Korea's division: if any country should have been divided it was Japan (like Germany, an aggressor). There was no internal pretext for dividing Korea, either: the thirty-eighth parallel was a line never noticed by the people of, say, Kaesong, the Koyro capitol, which the parallel cut in half. And then it became the only line that mattered to Koreans, a boundary to be removed by any means necessary. The political and ideological division we associate with the Cold War were the reasons for Korea's division; they came early to Korea, before the onset of the global Cold War, and today they outlast the end of the Cold War everywhere else.[9]

B. The Cold War Years

The United States was slow to understand its role on the Korean Peninsula. While the Soviet Union was busy occupying the North and providing funding and training while outfitting a formidable army, the United States was focused elsewhere, particularly in Japan and Germany, and as such did not put occupation troops into South Korea until September 1945, one month after the war ended. By this time, the Soviet Union was already establishing dominance in the North, restricting movement to and from its sector. It also was setting up an economic system which restricted access to the

---

[9] Bruce Cummings, *Korea's Place in the Sun: A Modern History* (New York: W.W. Norton, 1997), 87.

southern portion of the peninsula, further isolating Koreans in the north from countrymen in the south.[10]

From 1945 to 1950, various political solutions attempting to unite the peninsula were explored. A joint Soviet-American Commission was established in December 1945. This commission met periodically to discuss unification, but no solution was found. The Soviet Union had no intention of allowing a united but unfriendly government to take root in Korea.[11] Understanding this, in September 1947 the United States submitted the issue of the Korean peninsula to the United Nations for resolution, but none was to be found in this newly formed political body either. In 1948, two separate nations were officially formed in Korea. Eventually, each war power redeployed its troops – the Soviets in 1948 and the United States in 1949. At the time, the South Koreans were far from an adequately trained military force compared to the North Koreans forces. With domestic post-war politics demanding a quick downsizing of the United States military, training and equipping a Korean army just was not a priority compared to countering the iron curtain falling over Europe.

It was not until the outbreak of the Korean War that the United States fully began to see the peninsula as strategically important. Despite threats of war going back to as far as 1946, the hostilities were a surprise to President Truman and his advisors. Many historians point to Secretary of State Dean Acheson's speech of 12 January 1950 regarding a United States defense perimeter in the Pacific, one which did not include Korea, as the impetus for Stalin giving North Korean leader Kim Il Sung the green light for invasion of the South. Stalin had previously held off Kim on a couple of occasions,

[10] Stueck, 26.
[11] Ibid., 25.

but signals from the United States regarding the strategic unimportance of Korea coupled with Chairman Mao's recently completed Communist struggle in China against the Chinese nationalists gave Stalin enough reasons to relent to his protégé. Despite his concurrence, Stalin made it clear to Kim that it was China he was to rely on if the Americans came to help the South Koreans.

Mao positioned China to support North Korea for a variety of reasons. First, Mao considered the Korean War more than a threat to communist China sovereignty. He felt that it was the new regime's first opportunity to display to the world its ability to govern,[12] and Mao did not want to risk losing the support of the people of China when faced with an American threat across the Yalu River. Mao believed the Korean War would determine communist China's place in the world order. Additionally, Taiwan was a fresh topic among the world community, and Mao did not want to seem reluctant to counter world opinion when it was in China's strategic interests to do so.[13]

The horror of the Korean War was one piece of the Cold War which by now was in full bloom across the European Continent. These new Cold War security commitments, including one to South Korea, pushed the United States away from disarmament and toward policies centered on stopping Soviet aggression. South Korea, for its part, became a symbol of anti-communism, so much so that the United States eventually established a four star military command on South Korean soil in addition to providing security under United Nations mandates. In the end, the newly formed DPRK became a willing client state of the USSR, with South Korea developing the same relationship to the United States. As a result, the sides in Northeastern Asia in a global

---

[12] Jian Chen, *China's Road to the Korean War* (New York: Columbia University Press, 1994), 128.
[13] Kitty Tam, "China's Intervention in the Korean War," *The Brownstone Journal* Vol. VII, no. 1 (Spring 1998): 16-17.

struggle between communism and democracy were drawn – the United States and South Korea would stare down the USSR, China, and North Korea for most of the second half of the 20th century.

C. DPRK International Relations Post Cold War

With the end of the Cold War in 1991, North Korea could no longer count on the Soviet Union for guaranteed economic support, humanitarian relief, and security protection. With that needed security requirement in mind, the United States Government feared North Korea would begin a nuclear weapons program despite signing the Treaty on the Non-Proliferation of Nuclear Weapons (NPT) in 1985. The NPT is an international treaty with the purpose of preventing the spread of nuclear weapons while promoting the use of peaceful nuclear energy. It also establishes a safeguards system under the auspices of the International Atomic Energy Association (IAEA). These safeguards are used to ensure treaty compliance among the non-nuclear members. Suspicions arose because North Korea had forbidden the IAEA from conducting treaty-required on-site inspections of peaceful nuclear facilities, specifically the Yongbyon nuclear complex. Those fears were confirmed in 1989 when United States spy satellites spotted increased construction activities at the Yongbyon complex consistent with the early production stages of an atomic weapon.[14]

South Korea viewed the end of the Cold War as an opportunity to engage North Korea on a variety of issues. Specifically, President Roh Tae Woo called for increased contact with North Korea in international forums. A follow-up speech to the United

---

[14] *Kim's Nuclear Gamble* (Frontline: Public Broadcasting System, accessed 15 January 2007), available from http://www.pbs.org/wgbh/pages/frontline/frontline/shows/kim; Internet.

Nations General Assembly saw Roh offer to discuss security issues with North Korea bilaterally for the first time ever.[15] In September of 1990, North and South Korean officials met in Seoul. These minister-level meetings were the first of eight such meetings to take place, resulting in two agreements between the two adversaries. The first accord was the Agreement on Reconciliation, Nonaggression, Exchanges, and Cooperation (the Basic Agreement). The second one was the Declaration on the Denuclearization of the Korea Peninsula (the Joint Declaration).

The Joint Declaration, signed on 31 December 1991, "forbade both sides to test, manufacture, produce, receive, possess, store, deploy, or use nuclear weapons and forbade the possession of nuclear reprocessing and uranium enrichment facilities."[16] In March 1992 both sides agreed to form a Joint Nuclear Control Commission (JNCC) between North Korea and South Korea in order to verify compliance with the Joint Declaration. The JNCC never reached the implementation stage though, as the participants could not reach compromise on an inspection system agreeable to both nations. Prior to the JNCC formation, North Korea signed a nuclear safeguards agreement with the International Atomic Energy Agency (IAEA) in January 1992, establishing an inspection regime to begin in June 1992.

Despite both sets of agreements - one bilateral with South Korea and one internationally with the IAEA – serious inspections of North Korea's nuclear facilities never materialized. Pyongyang quickly began refusing the IAEA access to various inspection sites and less than a year after the fledgling inspection process began, North

---

[15] U.S. State Department, *Background Note: North Korea* (Bureau of East Asian and Pacific Affairs, October 2006, accessed 14 January 2007); available from http://www.state.gov/r/pa/ei/bgn/2792.htm; Internet.

[16] Ibid.

Korea announced its intention to withdraw from the NPT. Soon afterwards, the team leader from the IAEA, Hans Blix, announced he was unable to provide verification that North Korea was adhering to the NPT.[17]

The following year was to be one dominated by the nuclear issue in North Korea. Bilateral negotiation between Pyongyang and Washington concerning North Korea's nuclear programs were at a standstill. Pyongyang insisted it had every right to refuel its nuclear reactor at Yongbyon and to reprocess the fuel from the reactor to produce weapons grade nuclear material. Despite Washington's repeated declarations to Pyongyang to refrain from doing just that, North Korea began the process in April 1994. President Clinton, while working with the United Nations in an effort to impose sanctions, considered a variety of military options to stop North Korea. All were eventually deemed too risky, as the top United States military commander in Korea, General Gary Luck, estimated that nearly one million people would die on the peninsula if all-out war broke out.[18] Armed conflict was a concern because Kim Il Sung declared any sanctions imposed would be considered an act of war. In addition, he declared North Korea to now be in a "state of semi-war."[19]

It was at this point that former President Jimmy Carter became involved. The impetus for Carter's involvement was his longtime friend James Laney – the United States Ambassador to South Korea in 1994. Laney's concerns for the situation prompted

---

[17] Marion Creekmore, Jr., *A Moment of Crisis: Jimmy Carter, The Power of a Peacemaker, and North Korea's Nuclear Ambitions* (New York: Public Affairs, 2006), 36.
[18] James T. Laney and Jason T. Stapleton, "How to deal with North Korea," *Foreign Affairs* Vol. 82 no. 2, (March/April 2003), accessed 13 February 2007; available from http://www.foreignaffairs.org/20030301faessay10336/james-t-laney-jason-t-shaplen/how-to-deal-with-north-korea.html; Internet.
[19] C. Kenneth Quinomes, review of *A Moment of Crisis: Jimmy Carter, The Power of a Peacemaker, and North Korea's Nuclear Ambitions,* by Marion Creekmore, Jr., *Arms Control Association* (December 2006) accessed 10 January 2007, available from http://www.armscontrol.org/act/2006_12/BookReview.asp; Internet.

Carter to prepare for direct talks with Pyongyang. Despite a small faction within the Clinton Administration opposing Carter's intervention, he did meet with Kim Il Sung, though as a private citizen, and not as a direct representative of the United States Government. It was Carter's efforts that eventually lead to the DPRK-US 1994 Agreed Framework.

D. 1994 Agreed Framework and Clinton Administration Efforts

The 1994 Agreed Framework was not a treaty or a contract. It was just what it was titled – an agreed framework for North Korea and the United States to use to move forward regarding North Korea's adherence to the NPT and the future of its nuclear facilities. The Framework, only four pages long, discussed four major issues: North Korea's nuclear reactors, political and economic relations, a nuclear-free Korean peninsula, and the international nuclear non proliferation regime. The crux of the agreement centered on the nuclear reactor piece.

The agreement stated North Korea will "freeze its graphite-moderated reactors and related facilities and will eventually dismantle these reactors and related facilities."[20] North Korea also agreed to work with the United States to find a safe storage facility for all spent nuclear waste which could be used to fabricate nuclear weapons and to resume an IAEA inspection regime.

In return, the United States agreed to lead the international community in building two light water reactors and in developing alternative nuclear energy for the DPRK – a nuclear energy process that could not be modified into a weapons producing process.

---

[20] The Korean Peninsula Energy Development Organization, *Agreed Framework Between The United States of America and The Democratic People's Republic of Korea,* Geneva, 21 October 1994, Section I.3.

The international consortium referenced in the Agreed Framework eventually became the Korean Peninsula Energy Development Organization (KEDO). Washington also agreed to lead the international community in providing energy to North Korea to replace that which was lost when North Korea shut down its nuclear facilities.

The Agreed Framework was not met favorably in the United States. After Kim Il Sung died of a heart attack in July 1994 and was replaced by his son, Kim Jong Il, many in Congress were unhappy that America seemed to acquiesce to the new North Korean dictator. Since the agreement was not a treaty and not officially submitted to Congress for ratification, there was no requirement for the Republican-led Congress to fund the provisions within it. As such, it languished in the diplomatic quagmire of partisan politics, and the KEDO agreements were not fulfilled.

Despite slow progress on access issues related to a suspected nuclear underground site in Kumchang-ni, President Clinton still attempted to negotiate a settlement with North Korea as his term was coming to a close. The two countries began new negotiations in May 2000 as part of an official United States policy review towards the DPRK. These discussions paved the way for Secretary of State Madeleine Albright to visit North Korea in October 2000 and to meet personally with Pyongyang's leader. However, diplomatic efforts in the Israel-Palestinian peace process pushed the DPRK issue to the side temporarily, and the Clinton Administration efforts at settlement with Pyongyang ran out of time. Resolving the North Korean nuclear program issue would be left to the incoming Bush Administration.

E. Bush Administration Policy and the Six-Party Talks

Less than two months after President Bush took office in January 2001, South Korean President Kim Dae Jung arrived in Washington to discuss United States Government policy towards the Korean peninsula. He was also there to brief President Bush on South Korea's "Sunshine Policy" towards North Korea – a soft line approach towards reaching regional goals with Pyongyang. President Kim must have been hopeful of a harmonious reception, because on the day of the visit, Secretary of State Colin Powell was quoted as saying, "We do plan to engage with North Korea and to pick up where President Clinton and his administration left off."[21]

However, following the Clinton Administration policy was not what President Bush had in mind. He had no intention of possibly visiting North Korea for a summit in an effort to build on the recent 2000 talks, and publicly asserted that the Secretary of State went too far in his remarks. In his meeting with Kim Dae Jung, President Bush asserted his skepticism for any previous agreements with North Korea and stated any future "deal with North Korea would require complete verification of North Korea promises."[22] In June 2001, the Bush Administration officially stopped the nuclear and missile talks with the DPRK, citing the need to review policy towards Kim Jong Il's regime.

Seven months later in January 2002, North Korea found itself together with Iraq and Iran labeled as the "Axis of Evil" as the United States reacted to the September 11th terrorist attacks. Discussions with North Korea became subordinate to the broader Global War on Terrorism, and delegations did not meet formally again until October

[21] James Mann, *Rise of the Vulcans* (New York: Penguin Books, 2004), 277.
[22] Ibid., 278.

2002. It was during these meetings that Assistant Secretary of State for East Asian and Pacific Affairs James A. Kelly confronted North Korea concerning a covert DPRK uranium enrichment program that U.S. officials suspected was in operation. Shockingly, North Korea acknowledged the program, and confirmed that it violated the NPT and the 1994 Agreed Framework. It was at this meeting that a new American policy regarding North Korea was promulgated, one which stated the DPRK must terminate all nuclear weapons grade programs before there would be any movement on bilateral discussions or normalized relations. Shortly after these meetings concluded, North Korea changed course and denied the existence of the uranium enrichment program to the world community. However, as a result of the DPRK uranium enrichment admission, KEDO officially suspended all fuel shipments to North Korea.

North Korea then began to remove safeguards which had been in place as a result of the 1994 Agreed Framework. It revitalized its Yongbyon nuclear facilities, banned IAEA inspectors, removed all United Nations monitoring equipment, resumed processing weapons grade nuclear material, and announced its withdrawal from the NPT.[23] To counter these actions, the United States proposed a multilateral exchange on the North Korean nuclear issue.

North Korea opposed a multilateral process, insisting instead on bilateral talks directly with the United States. China eventually headed an effort to bring North Korea to the negotiating table. After a preliminary session in April 2003 between China, North Korea, and the United States, Japan, Russian and South Korea were invited to Beijing for the first Six-Party Talks in August 2003. President Bush has maintained that this is the

---

[23] U.S. State Department, *Background Note: North Korea* (Washington D.C.: Bureau of East Asian and Pacific Affairs, October 2006, accessed 14 January 2007); available from http://www.state.gov/r/pa/ei/bgn/2792.htm; Internet.

best forum for negotiations, as the situation should be resolved with input from all regional actors. The stated goal of the Six-Party talks is to resolve four peninsula-based issues: DPRK nuclear proliferation, ballistic missiles, refugees, and reunification of the two Koreas. However, over time three of the goals have moved to the background in favor of one main focus of effort for the Bush Administration – the complete irreversible and verifiable disarmament of North Korea's nuclear weapons program.

The first set of talks produced little of consequence. North Korea insisted it would abandon its nuclear program if the United States provided a security guarantee, energy aid and assistance, and diplomatic recognition. The United States in turn insisted on a verifiable end to Pyongyang's nuclear program. The second round of talks was then scheduled for February 2004.

The February meetings saw no concrete results, but the United States was encouraged by the dialogue and agreed to a third round, to be completed no later than June 2004. It was in this third meeting that the Bush Administration "tabled a comprehensive and substantive proposal aimed at resolving the nuclear issue."[24] Many viewed the United States sponsored proposal as a small concession to the other players in the Six-Party Talks, as Washington set forth this proposal before a complete and verifiable stop to the DPRK nuclear program. The proposal was enough to get North Korea to agree to further talks, and a fourth round was scheduled for Beijing in September 2004.

The fourth round of talks did not materialize on time as North Korea refused to return to the bargaining table and instead began to issue a series of threatening statements regarding the talks and its nuclear program. After much diplomatic wrangling by many

---

[24] Ibid.

parties, North Korea did finally sit down to negotiate in the summer of 2005. This two month session produced a Joint Statement of Principles, in which all six parties agreed to the goal of verifiable denuclearization of the Korea Peninsula.[25] North Korea agreed to eventual compliance with the NPT and a return to the IAEA safeguard routine. Other nations present agreed to provide energy and economic aid, and the United States agreed to review policy concerning recognition of North Korea.

Despite a fifth and sixth round of talks in November 2005 and December 2006 respectively, implementation of the Joint Statement of Principles did not occur. The DPRK continued to insist on expanding the talks to include bilateral issues of concern with the United States, and publicly Washington insisted on maintaining the current agenda.

February 2007 saw a potential breakthrough to the stalemate. The Six-Party Talks reconvened in Beijing, and common ground was found quickly among the participants. An agreement was reached whereby North Korea would dismantle its nuclear program and shut down its nuclear facilities in exchange for heavy fuel oil aid. Other diplomatic measures were included as well, but it is unknown if this tentative deal will be implemented by Pyongyang, or whether it will stagnate much like the September 2005 Joint Statement of Principles.

Despite periodic and repeated rhetoric about new openings and mutually agreed upon ideas over the tenure of the Six-Party Talks, Washington had remained reluctant to capitalize on openings by conducting bilateral negotiations. As the North Korean

[25] U.S. State Department, *Joint Statement of the Fourth Round of the Six-Party Talks* (Washington D.C.: Bureau of Public Affairs, 19 September 2005, accessed 23 October 2006); available from http://www.state.gov/r/pa/prs/ps/2005/53490.htm; Internet.

situation worsened throughout the summer and fall of 2006, Secretary of State Rice pressed President Bush to allow Assistant Secretary of State for East Asia Christopher Hill to conduct one-on-one discussions with Kim Kye Gwan, Hill's North Korea counterpart. Following the nuclear test event in the fall of 2006, President Bush relented and agreed to a January 2007 meeting between the two diplomats in Berlin. It is this bilateral dialogue outside of the Six-Party Talks that became the foundation of the multilateral deal announced in Beijing the following month.[26]

[26] Jim Lobe, *Korea Deal Marks Big Victory for Realists* (Inter Press Service News Agency, 14 February 2007, accessed 14 February 2007), available from http://www.ipsnews.net/news.asp?idnews=36552; Internet.

III. REGIONAL INTERESTS IN THE SIX-PARTY TALKS

A close study of each participant in these multi-lateral talks reveals just how differently each country approaches the negotiations. As discussed above, the main goal of the Six-Party Talks is to resolve four issues: DPRK nuclear proliferation, DPRK ballistic missiles, DPRK refugees, and peninsula reunification. However, not all of the nations represented in the talks has an interest in finding common ground for each point of contention. Each country views the talks as a means to accomplish ends vested only in its interests, and in some cases those results may be opposed to those of the others present at the bargaining table. The competing interests discussed below naturally divide the participants into two lines of approach towards North Korea. It is these two diverging approaches which diminish the chances of finding a compromise agreeable to all parties.

A. Japan

Japanese concerns regarding North Korea center on nuclear proliferation and ballistic missiles.[27] However, the seriousness of these issues has recently taken a back seat to a bilateral impasse between the two countries - North Korea's admitted abduction of at least thirteen Japanese nationals in the 1970s and 1980s. These hostages were used to train North Korean espionage agents in Japanese language and culture skills. This hot button topic with Japanese voters has forced the government to domestically elevate the abductee question to equal footing with the DPRK nuclear issue, demanding resolution of both before relations can be formalized. Because the abduction of Japanese nationals is not included in the Six-Party Talks agenda, it has been a point of friction, possibly

---

[27] Park, 78.

contributing to slow the pace of multilateral talks. However, the slow progress may not be troubling to the Japanese, as it may be in the best interest of the Japanese to ensure there is no permanent solution.

For Tokyo, the current conflict with North Korea is the "perfect excuse"[28] to maintain the bilateral diplomatic slow dance which has manifested itself between the two former enemies over the course of the last decade. Japan and North Korea have been conducting periodic bilateral discussions since 2002. These continued negotiations outside of the accepted Beijing sponsored effort provides Tokyo a hedging strategy in case of an unlikely resolution to the Six-Party Talks - a hedge which would allow Tokyo to gain influence in any future reunified but uneasy Korea. As it stands now, a continued conflict without resolution is in Japan's best interest because it leads to three things desired in Tokyo: continued development and deployment of a United States theater missile defense system, motivation for constitutional reform, and continuing warming relations resulting in greater economic interdependence between South Korea and Japan.

Since 1945, the United States has provided for Japanese security. Inherent in that security was defense from land based missile threats, and since the end of the Cold War North Korea has been the primary provocateur in this area. A theater missile defense system developed by the United States military has been providing a level of security for the Japanese during this current crisis. However, if the threat in the area is removed – if Kim Jong Il gives up nuclear weapons and ballistic missiles – than it stands to reason that the United States could redeploy system elements to other Asian threat areas. In this case, the Japanese would be forced to spend more money on national defense if Tokyo

[28] East-West Center: Building an Asia Pacific Community, *EU Parliamentarian: Six-Party Talks Hostage to Differing Desires* (Honolulu, HI: East-West Center, 2006, accessed 24 October 2006); available from http://eastwestcenter.org/events-en-detail.asp?news_ID=353; Internet.

decided it required a missile shield of some sort. To do this, certainly more money would need to be spent on defense than the current 1% of GDP.[29] A shifting of money to defense would remove money from other vital areas – areas which support Japan's aging workforce and robust economy, the foundation of Japanese power today.

A second benefit for Tokyo stemming from the current conflict is the growing desire among politicians for a constitutional change. Article Nine of the Japanese Constitution states:

> Aspiring sincerely to an international peace based on justice and order, the Japanese people forever renounce war as a sovereign right of the nation and the threat or use of force as means of settling international disputes. In order to accomplish the aim of the preceding paragraph, land, sea, and air forces, as well as other war potential, will never be maintained. The right of belligerency of the state will not be recognized.[30]

Japan's interest in becoming a more influential state in the region and throughout the world mandates a more robust military.[31] Japan's military has grown steadily over time, but to truly develop a top-tier military, constitutional change is necessary. With current tensions, Prime Minister Abe, a hawkish member of the conservative Liberal Democratic Party, may be able to garner the public support needed to push reform through.

A final benefit is an economic one. In 1999, Japan became South Korea's leading intra-industry trading partner, a spot formerly held by the United States.[32] Even though the two countries still remain politically cool towards each other for historical reasons, the economic bonds forged between Japan and South Korea in the 1990s, specifically

---

[29] U.S. Defense Department, *Allied Contributions to the Common Defense* (Washington D.C., July 2003, accessed 19 February 2007); available from http://www.defenselink.mil/pubs/allied_contrib2003/allied2003_Chap_1.html; Internet.
[30] House of Councilors, *Constitution of Japan* (Tokyo: The National Diet of Japan, accessed 23 October 2006); available from http://www.sangiin.go.jp/eng/law/index.htm; Internet.
[31] Yun Duk Min, *Japan's Dual Approach Policy toward North Korea: Past, Present, and Future* (Social Service Research Council, July 2005, accessed 13 September 2006); available from http://northkorea.ssrc.org/Yun/pf; Internet.
[32] For specifics, see Taegi Kim, and Kim Hong Kee, "Korea's Bilateral Trade with Japan and the U.S.: A Comparative Study," *Seoul Journal of Economics,* Vol. 12 no. 3 (Fall 1999): 239-57.

during the Asian economic crisis, have contributed to the rise of a stable and democratic South Korea. This economic relationship, coupled with the rise of China and North Korea's rogue threat towards Japan, has allowed the two former adversaries to develop a warmer relationship, culminating in a summit between South Korean President Kim Dae Jung and Japanese Prime Minister Obuchi Keizo. During this summit Japan issued a written apology to South Korea for its occupation of Korea – something Japan has not done before or since, and something it has have never done for China or North Korea.[33] Japanese interests and desires in the Six-Party Talks will result in continued support to South Korea in order to maintain economic stability, hedging against a stronger DPRK and China.

B. Russia

Russia no longer holds the strong influential position on the Korean peninsula that it held during the Cold War. As such, it views the Six-Party Talks as an opportunity to influence peninsula decision makers to support the current format for negotiations. The multilateral approach favored by the Bush Administration is why Beijing initially invited Russia to be active participant; supporting the United States and Beijing diplomatically now is seen by Moscow as a means to promote its own long term economic and security interests in the area.[34] These talks are an important political tool for Russia as it attempts to create a burgeoning economic opportunity should crisis resolution come to fruition.

---

[33] Lam Peng Er, "Japan's Differing Approaches on the Apology Issue to China and South Korea," *American Asian Review (U.S.),* Vol. 20 no. 3 (Autumn 2002): 31-54.
[34] Philip C. Saunders, "What to Expect from the Six-Party Talks on the Korean Nuclear Crisis" (25 August 2003, accessed 13 September 2006); available from http://cns.miis.edu/pubs/week/030825.htm; Internet.

Moscow's position on nuclear weapons on the Korean Peninsula is clear. Russian Federation President Vladimir Putin has been quoted many times, stating "We are against the DPRK's having nuclear weapons."[35] That being said, despite recent concurrence with economic sanctions imposed by the United Nations Security Council in response to the DPRK nuclear test, within the Six-Party Talks agenda Russia does not generally support stiff measures against North Korea. Along with a nuclear weapon free peninsula, Russia supports full compliance with the Non-Proliferation Treaty, compliance with the 1994 Agreed Framework, a United States security guarantee for the DPRK, resumption of humanitarian and economic aid programs for the North Koreans, and the ever elusive constructive dialogue between all members of the Six-Party Talks.[36] Russia believes in the DPRK's right to possess nuclear technology for energy related purposes, contingent on its return to the NPT and full compliance with an IAEA inspection regime. With Russia looking for additional free market opportunities to bolster its own economy, it is quite possible Russia seeks an economic windfall from the stability conflict resolution would provide. Assisting the DPRK regime develop peaceful nuclear energy, or even selling them the technology, would give Russia an added boost, and quite possibly help gain it the additional influence in the region it has been lacking since the end of the Cold War.

Russia is the only entity at the bargaining table without a high priority interest in the talks,[37] but it looks forward to a large share in the peninsula economy. Already since the beginning of the talks, Russian has begun an undertaking to extend the Trans-Siberian

---

[35] Valery Denisov, "Nuclear Crisis on the Korean Peninsula," *International Affairs,* Vol. 50 no. 6 (2004): 47.
[36] Ibid., 48.
[37] Park, 78.

Railroad to North Korea. In 2005, Vladimir Putin decided to prioritize oil exports to China after extensive flirtations with Japan first. Despite siding with China, it would be easy to project future oil exports to others in this area; one can imagine a future where Russian oil readily flows through China and North Korea to South Korea and indeed Japan via a future extension of the North Korean piece of the trans-Siberian Railroad. The only obstacle to future economic development for Russia in Northeast Asia is the lack of a negotiated settlement.

C. China

A statement by Sha Zukang, China's former ambassador for arms control and disarmament affairs, issued on 22 October 2002, formed the basis for Chinese policy at the outset of the Six-Party Talks. In it, Sha stated, "Dialogue and consultation is the best way to reach consensus....We should recognize that North Korea has legitimate security concerns. We need to continue the dialogue and practice more patience to ensure that the Korean peninsula is free of nuclear weapons."[38] This broad agenda guideline, coupled with U.S. pressure for Beijing to take a more active role in the future of its rogue client state, allowed China to become the diplomatic leaders in the Six-Party Talks.

Nuclear proliferation and North Korean refugees are China's main concerns. Ironically, it views the proliferation issue with much less concern than it does the refugee issue. China has historically viewed U.S. alarm over the DPRK ballistic missile threat and now the nuclear proliferation threat as hollow and insignificant. China believes that these threats are nothing without significant advancements in guidance and delivery

---

[38] Park, 84.

systems, and Washington's protestations to the contrary have done little to change Beijing's skepticism. Chinese leaders do see proliferation of these technologies to non-state actors as a world-wide threat,[39] however Beijing's view of proliferation in North Korea is tied to the refugee issue in that it believes both crises can be resolved by providing for that country's security.

A North Korean refugee crisis would be disastrous for China. China is currently engaged in a country wide concept of *xiaokang* – the remaking of its society to one in which the majority of Chinese would be middle class citizens. The goal of this policy is for the Chinese to reach $3,000.00 per capita gross domestic product by 2020.[40] Since China is a signatory to international agreements on refugee treatment, any North Korean regime collapse resulting in a northward exodus of refugees would potentially cause Western non-governmental agencies to mobilize. China would be under enormous international pressure to allow these non-governmental organizations into China to assist with the care and feeding of the displaced North Koreans. Allowing the Western world into China, and the international press that would undoubtedly follow, would force China to abide by the refugee treaties to which they have agreed. Doing so may negatively affect the *xiaokang* policy of the Beijing government, as Chinese citizens could possibly see the advancements of the Western world, and understand that these advancements are caring for the refugees better during an emergency than Chinese citizens are treated all year round. The population's dismay may morph into a demand for quicker government

---

[39] Park, 83.

[40] Forrest Lee, *China Vows to Cut Short Red Tape* (Beijing: People's Daily, 10 January 2003, accessed 26 November 2006); available from http://english.people.com.cn/200301/10/eng20030110_109907.shtml; Internet.

action on the citizen's behalf, and may ultimately disrupt governmental actions in support of the *xiaokang* policy itself.

A Japanese military buildup is also a major concern for the Chinese. As discussed earlier, the North Korean threat to Japan may spur constitutional reform in Japan, allowing offensive military capability for the first time in decades. An increase in Japanese capability would cause alarm in Beijing, and could force it to increase military spending. Any shift in China's carefully orchestrated national budget could cause a negative reaction within its economy. With China's international economic interdependency, any decline affecting China would have global economic repercussions.

In the end, China prefers a negotiated settlement that allows for economic reforms in the DPRK that suits China's economic style and improves relations with bordering states. Having a strict communist neighbor to the south as a buffer between China and the Western-leaning South Korea is no longer a concern to Beijing because China now sees itself as having more in common economically with Seoul than Pyonyang.[41] Because a DPRK collapse and the resultant refugees is its biggest concern, China continues to provide the bulk of international economic assistance to the DPRK despite UN sanctions. China's long term goal is a nuclear free-peninsula, and in the short term it desires to diffuse escalation. Today's Beijing government understands the biggest obstacle to stability and future economic development in North Korea is quite possibly the current DPRK regime's "fight to win or die" mentality.[42]

---

[41] Rob Gifford, *China and Its Neighbors, Part 4, South Korea* (Washington D.C.: National Public Radio, 17 February 2004, accessed 26 November 2006); available from http://www.npr.org/templates/story/story.php?storyId=1680309; Internet.
[42] Anne Wu, "What China Whispers to North Korea," *The Washington Quarterly,* Vol. 28, no. 2 (Spring 2005): 43.

D. Republic of Korea

The Republic of Korea's stated priorities in the Six-Party Talks are Korean unification and the prevention of North Korean refugees. Both issues shape current South Korean policy. While it does desire a nuclear-free, less militaristic North Korea, South Korea is much more concerned with maintaining a stable security environment, and this would be threatened by a dynamic reunification or a refugee crisis. This overarching security concern is the backbone of President Roh Moo Hyun's "Peace and Prosperity Policy."

The "Peace and Prosperity Policy" is a continuation of the previous administration's "Sunshine Policy." This policy seeks to maintain the stability of North Korea through massive economic aid. It seeks to enhance North Korea's economy and to "expand nascent economic ties with Pyongyang to develop inter-Korean relations further."[43]

According to Glyn Ford, a British member of the European Union Parliament and a member of its Foreign Affairs committee who has been on ten diplomatic missions to North Korea, South Korea studied the Germany reunification process very thoroughly. As a result, South Korea believes it has no other choice but to contribute to the stability of the "10 million North Koreans within a seven days walk of Seoul."[44] Not doing so would contribute to the opposite affect – the gradual destabilization of North Korea and the eventually collapse of the Kim Jong Il regime.

---

[43] Park, 80.

[44] East-West Center: Building an Asia Pacific Community, *EU Parliamentarian: Six-Party Talks Hostage to Differing Desires* (Honolulu, HI: East-West Center, 2006, accessed 24 October 2006); available from http://eastwestcenter.org/events-en-detail.asp?news_ID=353; Internet.

The cost of sudden reunification resulting from North Korean regime collapse would cripple South Korea's economy. South Korea is very proud of its economic standing in Asia and the world, and indeed has developed at an amazing rate since its collapse in 1997-1998. It was during this time that the population began to vote in large numbers for more liberal politicians, ones able to generate foreign investment allowing for greater economic prosperity.[45] These same politicians also believed in greater human rights than the old conservative politicians, and the impact of these policies was felt throughout South Korea at all income levels. This political surge in popularity has allowed the liberals to maintain power, and any crisis affecting economic policy would undoubtedly affect the current administration's political popularity as well. Keeping North Korea stable not only is good economic sense for South Korea, but is politically a necessity if the current party is to maintain power.

E. Democratic People's Republic of Korea

North Korea's stated high priority interest items in the Six-Party Talks are nuclear weapons, Korean reunification, and refugee migration. However, Pyongyang's negotiating tactics during each round of talks centered on physical and economic security guarantees, preferably ones "codified in an internationally recognized treaty, that the United States will not harm it economically or militarily."[46] It is these economic and military guarantees which would give Kim Jong Il what he truly desires – to maintain the status quo, with him remaining in power.

---

[45] Thomas L. Friedman, *The Lexus and the Olive Tree* (New York: Anchor Books, 2000), 107.

[46] Esther Pan, *North Korea: The Current State of Play* (Council on Foreign Relations, 10 January 2004, accessed on 24 December 2006); available from http://www.cfr.org/publications/7836/north_korea.html; Internet.

To obtain these security guarantees, North Korea has stated that it is willing to give up its nuclear weapons technology, but Pyongyang also demands an energy source under its own control. Since agreement to complete irreversible verifiable disarmament is the main goal of the Six-Party Talks, one would believe that this is a great starting point for North Korea. However, having an energy supply that would be under North Korean control is, at times, the sticking point in negotiations. With North Korean fossil fuel energy infrastructure being in tatters after years of sanctions and economic poverty, a reliable source of power must be found. One solution is for North Korea to tie into the South Korean infrastructure, but North Korea is understandably skeptical about its power source under Seoul's control. The other option for the power demand in North Korea is nuclear power, but nuclear power under North Korean autonomous control is out of the question for the negotiators from other countries.[47] For others to be comfortable with nuclear power in North Korea, the DPRK would have to agree to constant inspection and administration by the United Nations IAEA.

North Korea's detonation of a nuclear device in October 2006 was a gamble for Pyongyang. Instead of immediately being recognized as a nuclear power, Kim Jong Il has seen his support erode from long-standing soft liners China and South Korea. While not fully backing hard line supporters Japan and the United States of America, both China and South Korea did support additional sanctions in the United Nations targeted at North Korea. Aid from South Korea was temporarily curtailed, and China publicly criticized its communist friends. Many felt that the Chinese government was embarrassed by North Korea's actions. Zhu Feng, professor of international studies at

---

[47] East-West Center: Building an Asia Pacific Community, *EU Parliamentarian: Six-Party Talks Hostage to Differing Desires* (Honolulu, HI: East-West Center, 2006, accessed 24 October 2006); available from http://eastwestcenter.org/events-en-detail.asp?news_ID=353; Internet.

Peking University, stated that it was "time for a new approach, because we just got humiliated." He went on to say that "we have been so good to North Korea, trying to make the right conditions for Kim Jong Il to abandon nuclear weapons in exchange for normalization....China's goodwill has been relentlessly wasted."[48] Instead of being recognized as an equal among nuclear powers, Pyongyang inadvertently created a bilateral political issue with its staunchest ally.

The nuclear test may have had one positive result. Though the Bush Administration is publicly praising the February 2007 Six-Party Talks agreement as a win for multilateralism, there are indications that the nuclear test pushed President Bush into allowing a bilateral exchange between diplomats from the DPRK and Washington. It is this January 2007 exchange that laid the groundwork for the current deal.[49]

A final but potentially lethal issue in the eyes of North Korea is the end of financial sanctions levied by the United States in response to suspected North Korean counterfeiting efforts of United States currency. In September 2005, the Bush Administration placed financial restrictions against companies in North Korea and various banks and financial institutions suspected of assisting North Korea with money laundering of American currency. Of particular interest to North Korea is the restrictions faced by a Macau-based bank which currently holds $24 million of North Korea's money. The DPRK is insisting that sanctions be lifted by the United States as part of any

---

[48] "North Korea's Political, Economic Gamble," *The Washington Post*, 10 October 2006, sec. A, p.12.
[49] Jim Lobe, *Korea Deal Marks Big Victory for Realists* (Inter Press Service News Agency, 14 February 2007, accessed 14 February 2007); available from http://www.ipsnews.net/news.asp?idnews=36552; Internet.

nuclear agreement. This issue is clearly a bilateral issue, and one that is not currently discussed in the Six-Party Talks.[50]

F. United States

United States policy regarding North Korea changed after September 11, 2001. While in office during his first eight months, the Bush Administration had given little thought to Kim Jong Il and his regime other than trying to curtail North Korea's nuclear and ballistic missile proliferation efforts. All of that changed with the most dramatic terrorist attack ever on American soil, and the subsequent "Axis of Evil" labeling. Before this statement, the North Korean nuclear issue was not directly or indirectly associated with the Global War on Terrorism. While the Bush Administration has attempted to link terrorism to North Korea, the Six-Party Talks process has not centered on possible terrorist threats from North Korea. Its focus has continued to be North Korea's efforts at regional instability.

The United States approached the Six-Party Talks with nuclear proliferation and ballistic missiles as its primary focus of effort. The Bush Administration has maintained a hard line negotiating policy, publicly stating that the DPRK must agree to dismantle its nuclear arsenal and facilities before any other negotiations could even begin. Ultimately, the Bush Administration was in favor of regime change, but this policy was in direct conflict with South Korea's position that stability in the region was required in order to prevent a refugee crisis on the peninsula.

---

[50] "US tables North Korea proposal," *BBC News/Asia Pacific*, (London: BBC News, 20 December 2006, accessed 27 December 2006); available from http://news.bbc.co.uk/1/low/world/asia-pacific/6192323.stm; Internet.

After four rounds of negotiations, North Korea finally agreed to the nuclear demands of the United States and other nations involved in the Six-Party Talks, and a joint statement was issued on September 19, 2005. To date, no consensus has been reached on how to best implement this agreement, as North Korea insists any implementation of that accord must be tied to the United States lifting financial sanctions levied on the financial institutions discussed above. In preparation for the round of Six-Party Talks in December 2006, the United States stated publicly that it was willing to consider North Korea's demand concerning sanctions removal, but North Korea must revive the 2005 agreement and seriously discuss implementation.[51] The February 2007 agreement delineated a 30 day review of United States financial and economic sanctions, and the United States did indeed lift restrictions after the review allowing North Korea access to its funds from Macau based financial institutions. Time will tell if other bilateral issues, originally outside of the scope of the Six-Party Talks, will have any negative affect on all involved.

G. Summary

As seen from the discussion above, the nations involved in these talks have separate competing agendas. This sampling of issues involving the six nations involved in these multilateral talks clearly shows that each country has its own set of priorities, and therefore each government lobbies for resolution based on those competing interests. The participants have clearly landed in two separate camps – one a hard line camp (United States and Japan) and the other a soft approach camp (Russia, China, and South

[51]"US tables North Korea proposal," *BBC News/Asia Pacific* (London: BBC News, 20 December 2006, accessed 27 December 2006); available from http://news.bbc.co.uk/1/low/world/asia-pacific/6192323.stm; Internet.

Korea). Despite the United States hard line approach, North Korea still remains a distant thought when compared to the Global War on Terrorism. China has expressed frustration with the United States' unwillingness to provide diplomatic participation at the same level as China (China provides a Vice-Foreign Minister, the United States provides an Assistant Secretary of State), and the United States is frustrated with China's failure to provide tangible stepped-up pressure on its communist neighbor to the south. To some degree, the multilateral approach to the Six-Party Talks has been slowed by the competing interests of those involved. The policy coordination between the chief negotiating countries has been challenging as neither side agrees to the approach needed to solve the crisis. Both sides look to history to support competing approaches to North Korean nuclear disarmament. China and its allies support the Ukrainian approach. The United States and Japan support the Libyan approach. The next chapter will take a closer look at both case studies, and review South Africa's decision to voluntarily give up nuclear weapons.

IV. DISAVOWED NUCLEAR PROGRAMS

To understand the motivation of states who renounce nuclear weapons, various case studies must be analyzed. Libya and Ukraine each decided to forego nuclear weapons programs, a favorable position to the rest of the world but one which came about from very different beginnings for each country. South Africa is the only country in history to give up nuclear weapons after having already independently developing them. Knowing these countries' rationale for disarmament may provide an understanding that can be applied to the North Korean dilemma.

A. The Socialist People's Libyan Arab Jamahiriya (Libya)

Unknown to the world at large and shortly before the United States led invasion of Iraq in March 2003, the leader of Libya, Colonel Mu'ammar al-Qadhdhafi, authorized his personal representatives to contact President Bush and British Prime Minister Tony Blair concerning Libya's Weapons of Mass Destruction (WMD) programs. After years of enduring United Nations sanctions concurrent with years of building a robust but covert nuclear weapon program, Qadhdhafi was now openly discussing the dismantling of all Libyan WMD programs.

The history of Libya's nuclear weapons program is storied. King Idris of Libya signed the Treaty on the Non-Proliferation of Nuclear Weapons (NPT) in 1968. However, he was overthrown in a coup in 1969. Colonel Mu'ammar al-Qadhdhafi became Libya's new leader with a power base that was staunchly anti-Israel. It was this anti-Israeli sentiment that became the driving influence in launching a chemical and biological weapons program – the poor man's atomic bomb – and a subsequent nuclear weapons program.[52]

Libya began its nuclear program in earnest in 1970 immediately following the coup that brought Qadhdhafi to power. Overtures to foreign governments were sometimes successful – Libya did not have the technological capabilities to begin a program on its own – and soon there was a documented nuclear program relationship with Pakistan. Evidence gathered by the IAEA now shows that Libya was exploring both uranium and plutonium based weapons, and was able to import a significant amount of uranium ore concentrate from French-controlled mines in Niger. Libya admitted it did not declare all of the imports, and as such was able to conduct covert nuclear activities outside of IAEA safeguards with more than 1200 metric tons of uranium ore concentrate.[53]

Tripoli's ratification of the NPT in 1975 and agreement to IAEA safeguards surrounding nuclear energy related activities in 1980 did not stall efforts to build a covert nuclear capability. Throughout the 1980s Libya continued its attempts to purchase technological facilities in order to enrich uranium. It did in fact obtain a "pilot-scale uranium conversion facility in 1984."[54] While the country conducted uranium conversion experiments throughout the 1980s, it kept this facility inactive until 1998. Libya continued its technological imports through Pakistan in the 1990s, and ended up being the recipient of much nuclear related aid through Dr. A.Q. Khan, the father of the

---

[52] Joshua Sinai, "Libya's Pursuit of Weapons of Mass Destruction," *The Nonproliferation Review* (Spring-Summer 1997): 92.
[53] "Libya Country Profile," *Nuclear Threat Initiative* (Monterey Institute of International Studies: Center for Nonproliferation Studies, November 2006, accessed 2 January 2007); available from http://www.nti.org/e_research/profiles/Libya.html; Internet.
[54] Ibid.

Pakistani nuclear program and noted nuclear proliferation criminal who has aided programs in Libya, Iran and North Korea.

Nuclear efforts in Libya intensified in late 2000, culminating in the receipt of nuclear grade centrifuges. While not ever being capable of developing weapons grade uranium, Libya was moving forward with a geographically diversified program when Qadhdhafi reversed course and contacted Western officials with an offer to desist. Even while discussing the future renunciation of WMD, Libya continued to import technology capable of making the world's most powerful weapons.

Qadhdhafi's initial contacts with the United States and Britain were motivated by the desire to have economic sanctions lifted. Libya had endured 30 years of oil export sanctions which severely limited its economic growth. The additional cost of the WMD program itself also dampened governmental spending in domestic programs helpful to all Libyans. In addition to the economic concerns, Qadhdhafi had a strong and growing desire to return Libya to normal relations with the rest of the world. The leader understood normalization would only occur upon the elimination of WMD programs. Finally, one can surmise that Libya was watching world events, and did not want to experience the same fate of Saddam Hussein and Iraq.

Libya is the best example of success to support the hard line approach with North Korea. Libya endured decades of economic and political isolation from the world community in the form of sanctions due to terrorist activities and other indiscretions, similar to the DPRK. According to the Bush Administration, it was this isolation that pushed Libya to confront its past and renounce terrorism, take full responsibility for terrorist attacks it conducted, and come clean on its WMD program. It is this same path that many in the

United States and Japan believe should be followed when dealing with the rogue regime of North Korea. Indeed the Bush Administration had insisted on the Libyan approach to North Korean negotiations even before that approach was so dubbed.

B. Ukraine

With the fall of the Soviet Union in 1991, Ukraine suddenly found itself as one of four former Soviet Republics with strategic and tactical nuclear weapons on its soil. Along with Russia, Kazakhstan and Belarus, Ukraine was faced with a decision that could potentially decide its fate as an independent nation - what to do with these weapons.

Initially it was decided that joint control among nuclear nations within the newly formed Commonwealth of Independent States, which included Russia, Ukraine, Kazakhstan, and Belarus, would be the best way to maintain accountability of nuclear weapons. Russia, as the seat of the former Soviet Union, would still independently hold all launch codes for the weapons, leaving the leaders of Ukraine, Belarus and Kazakhstan unable to launch nuclear weapons without consensus from the Russian President. In fact, according to a 1996 Congressional Research Service Report, President Yeltsin agreed to consult the leaders of the other republics before launching weapons from Ukraine, Belarus or Kazakhstan, if needed. None of the leaders of these three countries requested unilateral operational control of weapons deployed to their newly independent countries.[55]

[55] Amy F. Woolf, *91144: Nuclear Weapons in the Former Soviet Union: Location, Command, and Control* (Congressional Research Service Reports: Foreign Affairs and National Defense Division, 27 November 1996, accessed 2 January 2007); available from http://www.fas.org/spp/starwars/crs/91-144.htm; Internet.

Joint control of nuclear missiles ended in the summer of 1993 when a new permanent agreement could not be reached. The strategic launch codes were transferred to the Russian Defense Minister from the Russian military, once again confirming that the nuclear weapons in question were under the political control of the Russian leadership irregardless of where the weapon was physically located. Soon Ukrainian and Russian officials could not agree on the administrative control of the weapons. Ukraine insisted it was responsible for administrative actions and troop levels for all weapons on its soil, but Russian disagreed and maintained that the Ukrainian actions violated its decree to become a nuclear-free state when it signed the Lisbon Protocol to START I in May 1992. Russian insisted that Ukraine did not have the necessary technological equipment to maintain the weapons.

It was during this time that some members of the Ukrainian government decided they wanted to retain some nuclear weapons in their country. This apparent change in policy, according to Ukraine, only applied to the missiles manufactured in Ukrainian facilities during the time of the Soviet Union, as property manufactured in Ukraine could be considered state property. In addition, "these weapons would have remained in a Soviet force under START, so Ukraine would not have to eliminate them to comply with the limits in START."[56]

After much political wrangling in 1993 and early 1994 during which Ukraine maintained a close negotiating stance with both the United States and Russia, Ukraine finally agreed to a trilateral declaration resulting in the elimination of all nuclear missiles and weapons. In addition, Ukraine agreed to and ratified the nuclear Non-Proliferation Treaty as a non-nuclear member. The driving force to this seemingly abrupt change in

---

[56] Ibid.

policy was the Ukrainian economy and Ukraine's desire for security. Because of its poor economic situation, Ukraine agreed to give up all claims to nuclear weapons in exchange for financial assistance and a security agreement. The financial assistance was provided by the United States to assist Ukraine in transporting all weapons to Russia. A memorandum guaranteeing Ukraine's security was signed by the United States, Russia, and, in addition, Great Britain.[57]

China, Russia, and both Koreas feel that the best way to find resolution with North Korea is to follow the Ukrainian approach and give Kim Jong Il what he has asking for – a security guarantee from the United States. At one time, the United States agreed to consider the Ukrainian approach. On 10 October 2003, Secretary of State Colin Powell publicly stated that the United States would be interested in a "written, open multilateral guarantee agreement" in order to move the deadlocked negotiations along.[58] This small diplomatic step was actually a great leap for the United States, which up until that time had been publicly stating that the DPRK must voluntarily renounce nuclear weapons first, as Libya had done seven months earlier.

C. The Republic of South Africa

South Africa is home to significant uranium deposits, and it was the discovery of this valuable commodity during World War II that pushed South Africa to begin its secret nuclear weapons program. However, it was not until 1959 that South Africa began a

---

[57] People's Daily, *The charisma of China's shuttle diplomacy reappears* (Beijing: People's Daily Online, 11 November 2003, accessed 9 January 2007); available from http://english.peopledaily.com.cn/200311/10/eng20031110_127987.shtml; Internet.
[58] Ibid.

large scale nuclear development program headed by the domestic Atomic Energy Board (AEB).[59]

Former members of the apartheid government in South Africa maintain that the program was initially peaceful, but the African National Congress believes the program was intended for weapons production from the beginning. The center of the program was an indigenously produced natural uranium reactor, and soon research began on uranium enrichment. Soon, the United States provided South Africa with a research reactor in Pelindaba, and in 1967 South Africa abandoned the use of its homegrown reactor program. Johannesburg continued with a uranium enrichment program.

Shortly thereafter, South Africa began programs to build peaceful nuclear explosives (PNEs), and subsequently constructed a uranium enrichment plant. Not being able to deny public scrutiny concerning the plant, South Africa announced the existence of nuclear technology, but denied anything other than peaceful uses of nuclear energy. It kept hidden its uranium enrichment facilities and its plans to produce weapons grade materials.

The culmination of South Africa's efforts was six nuclear weapons devices, and plans for a seventh. Motivation for the program came from security concerns. In a May 12, 2006 Newsweek interview, former President F. W. de Klerk explained that the bombs were "….to be used as a shield. It was built in the face of a definite threat, a definite strategy by the U.S.S.R., to directly or indirectly gain control of the whole of southern Africa…"[60]

---

[59] David Albright, *South Africa's Nuclear Weapons Program* (Institute for Science and International Security, 14 March 2001, accessed 20 January 2007); available at http://web.mit.edu/ssp/seminars/wed_archives_01spring/albright.htm; Internet.

The late 1980s found South Africa suddenly absent that security threat. War in Angola was over and Cuban forces had departed. The Soviet Union was in decline and focused on domestic issues instead of communist expansionism. In the same Newsweek article, de Klerk continued, "When I became president this threat changed in the sense that the Berlin Wall came down. Suddenly the U.S.S.R. was no longer this world power…we didn't need [the bomb], it had become a millstone around our neck…I wanted to return South Africa as soon as possible to the international arena, and I wanted to convince the rest of the world that we really were not playing with words…"[61] In the end, South Africa decided that its security was no longer threatened, and that being a responsible actor within the world was more important than possessing these nuclear weapons of mass destruction.

Within three years of its initial notification to the United Nations that it was willing to dismantle its nuclear weapons program, South Africa had adhered to the provisions of the NPT as a non-nuclear state. IAEA safeguards and inspection protocols remain in place today to ensure nuclear technology is used only for peaceful energy purposes.

D. Summary

South Africa, Libya, and Ukraine all gave up nuclear weapons programs for one reason: security. Each nation came to the conclusion via a different path. The lesson to be learned from these case studies is the positive effects of a stable national security environment. Libya wanted to enhance its security on the international stage and build

---

[60] Arlene Getz, *Q&A: F.W. de Klerk on Iran, Nukes* (Newsweek Web Exclusive, 12 May 2006, accessed 20 January 2007); available at http://www.msnbc.msn.com/id/12758097/site/newsweek; Internet.
[61] Ibid.

up its economy while having United Nations sanctions lifted. Ukraine suddenly found itself with nuclear weapons and decided it was better for its security to receive financial and economic aid to stabilize the new nation than to be a nuclear power. South Africa no longer felt threatened, and deemed itself secure without the burden of a nuclear arsenal.

Security is a powerful motivator. That motivation must be seriously explored by the Bush Administration in its negotiations with North Korea. Understanding an adversary's motivation is critical to establishing a viable policy across all elements of national power. Using all elements of national power in today's security environment is vital to meeting strategic objectives.

V. ELEMENTS OF NATIONAL POWER AND UNITED STATES' STRATEGY

The United States attempts to shape the strategic environment worldwide in an effort to meet strategic objectives nested in its national interests. Implementation of policy to support those strategic objectives is developed using elements of national power spread across the entire domain of the federal government. It is these elements of national power that the United States uses to carry out its policy regarding North Korea. When attempting to establish executable policy, it is necessary to thoroughly review and understand the elements to determine potential impacts of each.

A. The Elements of National Power

Four distinct elements of National Power shape American strategy. [62] Various agencies within the Executive Branch of the United States Government are charged with developing strategy and policy using these elements with very little mandatory coordination among agencies.

Of the four elements of National Power, Information is the one most difficult to define. Joint Publication 1 and other references continue to list Information as an element of National Power, but in today's governmental structure, Strategic Communication is poorly planned and executed. The United States Information Agency ceased to exist is 1999, and coordinated Strategic Communication from the government, effective or not, ended with its demise.

---

[62] *Joint Publication 1: Joint Warfare of the Armed Forces of the United States* (Washington D.C.: Joint Chiefs of Staff, 14 November 2000, v.

The current Bush Administration has recognized a need to address this issue. Former Presidential Advisor Karen Hughes has been appointed the Undersecretary of State for Public Affairs and Public Diplomacy. Despite the added attention, the Informational element of National Power remains a weak link.

A broad but powerful national element of power, the Economic arm is spread among a few agencies within the Executive Branch. The Office of Management and Budget is the lead agency regarding discretionary and non-discretionary governmental spending. The Federal Reserve Board provides policy on interest rates, and both the Department of State and Department of Commerce work on trade agreements and trade policy. The economic element of national power is vital for overseas and domestic stability.[63]

Under the purview of the Department of State, the Diplomatic element of National Power seeks to shape the international arena to favor policies of the United States. This is accomplished through a variety of negotiations (both bilateral and multi-lateral) with foreign governments, non-governmental organizations, the United Nations, and other governmental bodies.

Americans are most familiar with the Military element of National Power. Led by the Department of Defense, it is the element often seen on the nightly news, and is often the only element resourced in a chosen struggle. While on equal footing with the previous elements outlined above, the military element is the only one with standardized

[63] Office of Management and Budget, *FY-07 Budget* (Washington, DC: U.S. Government Printing Office, accessed 20 November 2006) available from http://www.whitehouse.gov/omb/pdf/Economy-07.pdf.; Internet.

planning and execution processes and the career staff functions capable of influencing a crisis in the short term. [64]

The Department of Defense has conducted extensive contingency planning at the tactical and operational levels vis-à-vis North Korea. These plans generally treat North Korea as a traditional Cold War adversary, ignoring trends in recent Department of Defense and United States Government strategic documents. A careful review of these strategic documents is required when deciding on the potency of the military element of national power regarding North Korea.

B. Strategic Documents

Two strategies published within the Department of Defense are derived from the National Security Strategy. These are the National Military Strategy (issued by the Chairman of the Joint Chiefs of Staff) and the National Defense Strategy (issued by the Secretary of Defense).

1. National Military Strategy (NMS)

Last published in May 2004, the NMS provides three priorities to the Armed Forces: winning the War on Terrorism, enhancing joint warfighting, and transforming for the future.[65] The body of work provides supporting documentation and commentary to support the Chairman's first stated priority – winning the Global War on Terrorism. A careful review of the entire document shows no direct reference to North Korea,

---

[64] Clark A. Murdock, *Beyond Goldwater-Nichols: Defense Reform for a New Strategic Era* (Washington, DC: Center for Strategic and International Studies, March 2004), 61.
[65] Richard B. Myers, *National Military Strategy of the United States of America"* (Washington, DC: Joint Chiefs of Staff, May 2004), iv.

though elements of the NMS can be inferred to mean the DPRK. Specifically, discussing possible air and missile attacks and reference to "swiftly defeating adversaries in overlapping campaigns"[66] conjures up images of the DPRK. However, the stated purpose of this published strategy is to deal with the Global War on Terrorism. The implied references to North Korea above can be linked to the overall Global War on Terrorism, not a traditional North Korean Army ground campaign. It does not specifically present North Korea as a traditional military threat.

2. National Defense Strategy (NDS)

This document was last published in March 2005 and "outlines an active, layered approach to the defense of the nation and its interests."[67] It is broken down into three chapters. These chapters are titled "America's Security in the 21st Century," "A Defense Strategy for the 21st Century," and "Desired Capabilities and Attributes."[68]

The first chapter of the NDS is the only area which specifically mentions North Korea. It states that the DPRK "at once poses *traditional, irregular,* and *catastrophic* [sic] challenges" as defined by the NDS.[69] Given that page 2 of the NDS also states "the U.S. military predominates in the world in *traditional* forms of warfare" and that "potential adversaries accordingly shift away from challenging the United States through *traditional* military action," the NDS implies that the threat from North Korea stems from *irregular* and *catastrophic* challenges.

---

[66] Ibid., 3.
[67] Donald H. Rumsfeld, *The National Defense Strategy of The United States of America* (Washington, DC: U.S. Government Printing Office, March 2005), iv.
[68] Ibid., ii, iv.
[69] Ibid., 2.

Both of these remaining challenges are specifically related to terrorism. The NDS refers to *irregular* methods as "terrorism and insurgency" and states "proliferation of WMD technology and expertise makes contending with *catastrophic* challenges an urgent priority."[70] Page 4 of the NDS defines Problem States as those that "will continue to undermine regional stability and threaten U.S. interests." The description of Problem States as ones that "commonly squander their resources to benefit ruling elites, their armed forces, or extremists clients" and ones that "may seek WMD or other destabilizing military capabilities"[71] strongly infers this paragraph is a direct reference to North Korea. If so, it implies that the Secretary of Defense believes that North Korea is less a *traditional* Cold War threat than a possible ally of the emerging world-wide terrorist threat.

While geographic Combatant Commanders do have operational and tactical plans on the shelf to counter a traditional North Korean military threat, a review of the above Department of Defense documents show that the civilian and military leaders of the Armed Forces believe North Korea is best dealt with as an emerging Global War on Terrorism threat. The Secretary of Defense states in the Foreword to the NDS that "We are confronting fundamentally different challenges from those faced by the American defense establishment in the Cold War and previous eras."[72] North Korea, the last vestige of the Cold War, is seen as less of a *traditional* threat, one which the United States is satisfied can be defeated conventionally, and more of an *irregular* and *catastrophic* threat.

---

[70] Ibid., 3.
[71] Ibid., 4.
[72] Rumsfeld, iii.

Additionally, the Chairman of the Joint Chiefs of Staff publishes a National Military Strategic Plan for the War on Terrorism,[73] but does not publish a National Strategic Plan for Lingering Cold War Threats. Terrorism is clearly the focus of the Department of Defense. With transformation continuing to make the Armed Forces a leaner, more agile force - one capable of success in the global commons - dealing with potential adversaries in the context of the Global War on Terrorism may help alleviate Department of Defense planning concerns for possible future conflicts with both asymmetrical threats and previous era conventional threats.

3. National Security Strategy (NSS)

The most recent NSS was published by President Bush in March 2006. Direct and implied references to the DPRK are found throughout the document. The most direct reference to North Korea is in the Chapter titled "Prevent Our Enemies from Threatening Us, Our Allies, and Our Friends with Weapons of Mass Destruction." [74] In it, the President characterizes the DPRK as a "serious nuclear proliferation challenge."[75] The commentary that follows discusses diplomatic approaches to the North Korean dilemma and lists many non-military concerns in addition to the missile and nuclear proliferation issues.

Implied references to North Korea throughout the NSS include discussing tyrannical and oppressive regimes, addressing regional conflicts through engagement, and forging relationships with members of the Six-Party Talks. At no point anywhere in

---

[73] Peter Pace, *National Military Strategic Plan for the War on Terrorism* (Washington DC: Joint Chiefs of Staff, 1 February 2006).
[74] George W. Bush, *The National Security Strategy of The United States of America* (Washington, DC: The White House, March 2006), 18.
[75] Ibid., 21.

the National Security Strategy is it implied that the solution to the North Korean impasse is solely throughout the use of the military arm of National Power. Thus, it can be concluded that the National Defense Strategy and the National Military Strategy were developed to support the Global War on Terrorism as the main focus of effort, and that military strategic thinking should be centered on that effort.

4. Quadrennial Defense Review (QDR)

Another important Department of Defense document which warrants review is the 2006 Quadrennial Defense Review (QDR). The Secretary of Defense states that the QDR "sets out where the Department of Defense currently is and the direction we believe it needs to go in fulfilling our responsibilities to the American people."[76]

While maintaining the armistice on the Korean peninsula is mentioned in the QDR, the only direct reference to North Korea is on page 32, where it discusses the DPRK's efforts surrounding weapons of mass destruction.[77] Many references to WMD proliferation and rogue states are made throughout the document, further implying that North Korea should be considered more as an emerging irregular threat than a traditional military threat. Further reinforcing this line of thought is the Secretary of Defense's Fiscal Year 2007 Posture Statement before the House Armed Services Committee. In this 27 page statement, Secretary Rumsfeld does not mention North Korea at all, but does make reference to threat scenarios involving rogue missiles and loose nuclear weapons.[78]

---

[76] Donald H. Rumsfeld, *Quadrennial Defense Review Report* (Washington, DC: U.S. Government Printing Office, 6 February 2006), iii.
[77] Ibid, 32.
[78] Statement of Secretary of Defense Donald H. Rumsfeld, FY 2007 Posture Statement before The House Armed Services Committee, 8 February 2006.

In his personal testimony discussing the QDR, it was terrorism, Iraq, preparing for the unexpected, and transformation that dominated. His justification for the Defense budget centered in these topics and did not mention North Korea. This testimony is evidence that strategic thinking would allow for the North Korean threat to be resolved by other than military means.

C. Summary

Reviewing the elements of National Power in context with published grand strategy documents from the Executive Branch provides a roadmap for the Bush Administration to engage North Korea. Though the military element of National Power is the arm most default to, it is clear from the NSS, NDS, and NMS that a traditional conflict with North Korea is not in line with United States Government strategic thinking. These documents clearly articulate the threat as terrorism, and classify North Korea as a threat that is both *irregular* and *catastrophic*. As such, the United States Government should look to other elements of National Power to engage the DPRK threat as it relates to the Global War on Terrorism – the prolifcration of Weapons of Mass Destruction.

Of the other three elements of National Power, neither the Informational nor the Economic arms will have impact in dealing with North Korea. North Korea has been a closed society for over fifty years, and is one of the last bastions of communism. Communications links with other countries are virtually non-existent. That, coupled with a lack of Strategic Communication from the U.S. Government, renders the Informational element of National Power impotent in this case. Impotent as well are any additional economic measures taken against North Korea. North Korea has been subject to various forms of sanctions for many years, and despite many hardships suffered by the North Korean people, the DPRK leadership refuses to take actions required to have sanctions lifted.

The remaining element of National Power is the Diplomatic element. The United States Government uses this element with North Korea, having been engaged with the DPRK within the Six-Party Talks since 2003. President Bush has been adamant about the need to engage North Korea multilaterally, with all regional actors involved. However, not all of the other players in the talks have taken the same stance, and each country involved has engaged North Korea bilaterally to resolve national issues or advance national economic policies.[79] The United States too should attempt to engage North Korea diplomatically in support of Global War on Terrorism goals.

Despite recent acquiescence to return to the Six-Party Talks, North Korea has always maintained its desire for face-to-face talks with the United States. Indeed, history has shown that direct dealings with Kim Jong Il resulted in a limited achievement of goals – accountability of DPRK fissile material by international inspectors. Within the Global War on Terrorism, the United States desires that accountability yet again. If direct engagement with North Korea is the mechanism that nets that goal, then nothing should stand in the way of accomplishment – not even President Bush's mantra that "the fundamental character of regimes matters."[80] If the United States is in fact in the "early years of a long struggle,"[81] then the Administration should indeed use all elements of National Power in that struggle. It is time to engage North Korea bilaterally as part of the

---

[79] Glyn Ford, *EU Parliamentarian: Six-Party Talks Hostage to Differing Desires* (Honolulu, HI: East-West Center, 2006, accessed 24 October 2006); available from http://eastwestcenter.org/events-en-detail.asp?news_ID=353; Internet.
[80] Bush, 1.
[81] Ibid.

greater Global War on Terrorism. Not doing so when the opportunities are there is a detriment to United States national security.

VI. ANALYSIS AND RECOMMENDATIONS

Overt bilateral engagement of North Korea would be a major policy shift for the Bush Administration. From the very beginning of President Bush's tenure in the White House, he has executed a North Korean negotiating policy that at times seems to be based more on emotion than realist politics. In an August 20, 2002 interview with Bob Woodward, President Bush acknowledged the passion he feels when forming policy about the future of North Korea. "I loath Kim Jong Il!" President Bush is quoted as saying to Woodward. President Bush noted that there would be "strategic ramifications" felt throughout the world if regime change occurred in North Korea, but that he felt a different issue was more pressing. The "immense suffering" felt by the North Korean people was more important than the instability that may occur from toppling Pyongyang. Despite his "passion" for the "starving people" of North Korea, President Bush did not have a cogent policy for dealing with the subject of his ire. By the time of this Woodward interview, President Bush's multilateralism policy towards North Korea was in its infancy stage, with the first discussions between the Bush Administration and North Korea occurring in October 2002.

This lack of Presidential urgency towards negotiations with North Korea is troubling. A Central Intelligence Agency (CIA) report from November 2002 confirmed North Korea's clandestine efforts to produce weapons grade uranium, and even before that it was apparent to members of Bush's team that North Korea was an international threat. In January 2002, the Undersecretary of State for Arms Control Josh Bolton reported that North Korea had an ongoing covert nuclear weapons program.[82] A former

[82] Seymour M. Hersh, *Chain of Command* (New York: Harper Collins Publishers, 2004) 307.

American intelligence official laments that "…they never had a sensible approach. The Administration was deeply, viciously ideological. When it came time to confront North Korea, we had no plan, no contact – nothing to negotiate with. You have to be in constant diplomatic contact, so you can engage and be in the strongest position to solve the problem." Solving the North Korean problem was far from the Bush Administration's agenda in 2002, as history has shown building a case for war with Iraq was priority number one. As such, policy floundered and a clear agenda was never developed. In the end, the Bush Administration decided it would not be "blackmailed" to the bargaining table, and tensions escalated between Pyongyang and Washington.[83]

Critics of Bush Administration DPRK policy point to the dubious nature of the CIA report as evidence that policymakers lacked a clear vision and only wanted to shape events on the peninsula to facilitate political needs. Throughout 2002, Washington saw a softening of the peninsula agenda by others, so much so that hard liner Japan was discussing the normalization of relations with North Korea without Washington knowledge or input. When faced with competing interests that conflicted with the "Axis of Evil" proclamation, detractors say Washington decided to release not fully vetted suspicions in an effort to shape Korean peninsula regional policy.[84]

Policy should not be based on emotion. Policy should be formed on a thorough understanding of history, regional interests, and the motivation of the actors involved. It should be articulated by published government strategies. Developing North Korean policy with an eye towards these issues will lead to a clearly defined, executable plan

---

[83] Ibid., 310.

[84] Jonathan D. Pollack, "The United States, North Korea, and The End of the Agreed Framework," *Naval War College Review,* Vol. LVI, no. 3 (Summer 2003), accessed 22 February 2007; available from http://www.nwc.navy.mil/press/Review/2003/Summer/art1-su3.htm; Internet.

designed to promote regional stability while achieving successes supporting the highest strategies of the United States Government.

A. Situation Analysis

1. History

The Korean people, and especially the North Koreans, have not had much of a history of self-determination. Japan forcibly annexed the Korean peninsula in 1910. The Japanese reign was especially harsh, and the Korean people suffered many atrocities at the hands of their neighbors to the east. The end of Japanese rule in 1945 did not bring freedom for the North Koreans, as governments were installed that fell in line with the communist thinking of Soviet leader Joseph Stalin. North Korea was a traditional Soviet satellite state that played by the rules of the Soviet Union. With the Korean War came increased Chinese sponsorship, albeit with continued influence from the Kremlin. Self-determination and a representative government system were not in the cards for the people of North Korea.

The Cold War ended in 1991, but the Cold War still plays out daily on the Korean peninsula. Despite the fall of the Soviet Union and the open market capitalist leanings of the Chinese, North Korea has maintained a hard line communist stance. Generations of North Koreans know nothing except the communist way of life. Without overt Soviet and Chinese patronage, Pyongyang has struggled to be an equal actor on the world stage. For the first time in modern history, North Korea is able to make independent decisions based on its own national interests.

Kim Jong Il has set policies in motion that push for the world community to deal with him as an international equal. After nearly 50 years of being a pawn in a worldwide game of chess followed by 10 more years of international isolation, Pyongyang's truest desires may be only to be treated like an equal. Negotiating bilaterally would elevate North Korea's diplomatic self esteem and possibly eliminate a point of friction between Washington and Pyongyang.

2. Regional Interests

As discussed in Chapter III, the actors of the Six-Party Talks have diverse interests. Not all of the players have the same motivation for being at the bargaining table. These divergent views may have contributed to the sluggish nature of the talks. The slow progress had caused some members of the international community to question the utility of such talks.

The United States does not recognize North Korea diplomatically and does not maintain an embassy in Pyongyang. President Bush has maintained that negotiating bilaterally with North Korea would legitimize the regime there. However, none of the other players involved in the nuclear disarmament talks have taken the same stance. Each country at the table engages North Korea bilaterally on a number of issues, ranging from human rights issues to economic aid to trade rights. The United States is the only country not to take advantage of a bilateral negotiating table to bargain in its own interests only. Engaging North Korea bilaterally, as North Korea has repeatedly requested, could help remove natural multilateral friction and allow for a negotiated settlement equally advantageous to both the citizens of North Korea and the United States.

3. Motivation

To denounce nuclear arms requires a tremendous sense of security based on other factors. As Chapter IV discussed, the motivation for disarmament takes many forms, but in the end the ultimate motivation is stability and security. If North Korea is to cease production of nuclear weapons and allow for verifiable inspections to confirm disarmament, certainly Pyongyang would expect something in return.

Pyongyang's demands of diplomatic recognition, a security guarantee, and energy aid is in concert with the desires of Libya, Ukraine, and South Africa. Each of these countries found stability and security more important than nuclear weapons. At the end of any negotiations, Kim Jong Il still wants to be leader of North Korea. Gaining diplomatic recognition from the United States as well as a security guarantee ensures his leadership survives in the international arena. Gaining energy aid in excess of current capacity would quell possible internal dissension by increasing North Korean quality of life. While doing so would also help Kim Jong Il maintain his grip on power, the overall benefit outweighs this disadvantage.

4. United States National Interests

United States Government negotiating policy regarding North Korea should be centered on United States strategic objectives, which are nested with United States national interests. The strategic analysis conducted in Chapter V supports an overarching grand strategy in support of the Global War on Terrorism. President Bush and future administrations should manage future relations with North Korea in support of strategic and operational objectives tied to that grand strategy. This should be the top priority of United States policy.

Two additional areas of national interest are tied to North Korea. The first issue is the prevention of hostilities on the peninsula – the outbreak of another Korean War. There are still approximately 27,500 United States military personnel stationed on the peninsula itself, and there are countless more stationed throughout the region. North Korea has a huge army with equally huge conventional weapons stockpiles in addition to its unknown number of nuclear weapons. War would trigger treaty requirements on both sides of the Korean peninsula's demilitarized zone, bringing the United States and China into the conflict immediately. One could surmise that Russia and Japan would enter the conflict as well in order to protect national interests. Politically and economically, the results would be catastrophic for all involved, and equally economically disastrous for others not involved as well.

The second additional area of national interest is a continued strong bond between the United States and the Republic of Korea. While many in the late 1940s thought the Korean peninsula held little strategic value, today its importance it magnified. Other than the island nation of Japan, South Korea is the only strategic ally the United States has in Northeast Asia. Having a footprint on the Asian continent is an important strategic necessity for the United States to maintain regional influence. As China works to be the next great superpower, it is critical for the United States to remain active locally in Asia so "China's rise to global prominence can be managed."[85]

B. Recommended United States Policy Regarding North Korea

1. Bilateral Negotiations

Negotiating bilaterally with North Korea will allow the United States to accomplish its nuclear non-proliferation objectives related to the Global War on Terrorism and maintain its national interests in the region without depending on other nations for strategic success.

Critics will bemoan direct negotiations with a brutal dictator, citing the legitimacy such talks would give to Kim Jong Il. Others will point to the need to keep other countries engaged to support regional stability. Both of these points are valid, but as President Bush stated in a September 2006 speech, the Global War on Terrorism "is the great ideological struggle of the 21st century -- and it is the calling of our generation."[86] If this Global War on Terrorism is truly generational, it should be the overarching grand strategy under which Washington nests every strategic and operational objective.

Legitimacy concerns are naïve and shortsighted. Negotiating with a brutal regime to support broader policy goals is nothing new for the United States. During the Cold War, administrations from Truman to George H.W. Bush talked with the Soviet Union bilaterally on a number of issues. Communism was seen as a threat, but policy makers none the less found direct negotiations as the best way to counter that threat. The fight

---

[85] Michael Elliott, "The Chinese Century," *Time*, January 22, 2007, 42.
[86] Speech by President George W. Bush, Capitol Hilton Hotel, Washington D.C., 5 September 2006; transcript accessed 10 February 2007; available from http://www.whitehouse.gov/news/releases/2006/09/20060905-4.html; Internet.

against Moscow's way of life was indeed a generational struggle similar to the "Long War" the United States now finds itself in. If direct negotiation is the instrument needed to support successful accomplishment of elements of the Global War on Terrorism, then the United States should not let ideology stand in the way. In addition, the bilateral talks that provided the foundation for the recent Six-Party Talks success should be seen as an opening for Washington in its efforts to stop nuclear proliferation within the greater context of the Global War on Terrorism.

Regional concerns can still be addressed via the Six-Party Talks agenda. Indeed, keeping the Six Party Talks active as a means to identify and resolve issues among all six actors is essential to maintaining stability in the area. Issues of Korean reunification and refugees are of vital interest to regional parties, but are not necessarily tied to any United States Global War on Terrorism strategic objective. The South Korean desire to enhance North Korea's quality of life with massive amounts of aid while attempting to modernize North Korea's economy supports the stability objectives all parties feel are vital to maintaining peace on the peninsula. Supporting the South Korean soft line policy gives legitimacy to the efforts while removing the hard line United States policy as a point of friction with Pyongyang.

The key to a viable stability construct lies with China. Along with supporting the Ukrainian approach to this issue, China has been covertly and overtly attempting to get Kim Jong Il to modify North Korea's economic structure to make Pyongyang mirror Socialist China. This would improve the North Korean economy and therefore promote stability.

North Korea has also riled Beijing with its bellicose nature. While Article VII of the Treaty of Friendship, Cooperation, and Mutual Assistance Between the People's Republic of China and the Democratic People's Republic of Korea states, "The present Treaty will remain in force until the Contracting Parties agree on its amendment or termination,"[87] China should make it clear to Pyongyang that future implementation will be defensive in nature only. Beijing must make it clear that it would come to Pyongyang's defense if attacked, but that North Korea should not expect China to rescue Pyongyang from government collapse or internal strife that results in South Korea taking governmental action north of the DMZ. The United States should covertly approach Beijing to address this issue within the Six-Party Talks. China then must pressure North Korea within the context of these talks to become a more economically open society in order to alleviate the economic stress that contributes to possible instability and eventual regime collapse. However, for the United States to expect China's cooperation, it should be prepared to follow through with tangible steps to promote the same desired effects.

2. Security Guarantee

Providing North Korea a written security guarantee would be that necessary step needed to convince China to take the steps discussed above. The security guarantee would also be an important building block to Global War on Terrorism based bilateral negotiations between the DPRK and United States on the subject of nuclear proliferation.

The recent Six-Party Talks agreement centered on Pyongyang's existing nuclear program and facilities, but it did not address the DPRK nuclear plutonium based weapons

---

[87] *Treaty of Friendship, Cooperation, and Mutual Assistance Between the People's Republic of China and the Democratic People's Republic of Korea,* accessed 10 October 2006, available from http://www.marxists.org/subject/china/documents/china_dprk.htm; Internet.

arsenal.[88] The United States should engage North Korea bilaterally in support of Global War on Terrorism nuclear proliferation objectives. One important step in this engagement is to remove the threat of preemptive invasion by the United States. North Korea has long maintained that America is an imminent threat requiring a strong deterrent. Removing that threat via a security guarantee could provide an impetus for dismantling the current DPRK stockpile under IAEA guidelines, and could possibly provide a framework for returning North Korea to the NPT.

There is little risk to a security guarantee from the United States' point of view. It would be clearly worded to become void in case of hostile aggression, allaying concerns of South Korea, Japan, and domestic critics. The guarantee would only be valid as long as North Korea continues following all Six-Party Talk agreements and all other elements of bilateral agreements reached with the United States.

3. Normalization of Relations

In addition to a security guarantee, the United States should normalize relations with North Korea and open an embassy in Pyongyang. Not doing so negatively impacts the strategic objectives tied to United States national interests. National interest dictates a continued presence in the Northeast Asian region to hedge against an increasingly strong China. Normalizing relations with the Kim Jong Il regime and building an American diplomatic presence in Pyongyang increases the United States footprint in the diplomatic, information, and economic elements of national power. Doing this while decreasing the

---

[88] Jim Lobe, *Korea Deal Marks Big Victory for Realists* (Inter Press Service News Agency, 14 February 2007, accessed 14 February 2007); available from http://www.ipsnews.net/news.asp?idnews=36552; Internet.

military footprint in South Korea could go a long way in gaining valuable trust needed in developing this new bilateral dialogue.

Neoconservative critics will argue that this diplomatic overture in a broader bilateral construct is nothing but appeasement towards North Korea. On the contrary, having a diplomatic presence, while a North Korea goal and a demand for talks, is not just a win for North Korea. Gaining insight through physical presence in North Korea is a valuable resource long neglected by many administrations. During the Cold War, the United States maintained embassies in many communist countries. These diplomatic missions were undoubtedly a valuable source of information while negotiating between East and West, and indeed played an important role in heading off major crises over the course of history.

4. Enhancement of Economic Aid and Infrastructure Support

The third tier to any bilateral negotiating effort would start with the enhancement of economic aid, including energy aid, provided to North Korea through the Six-Party Talks and KEDO construct. In addition to following through on United States commitments here, the American government should propose expanded economic aid and food support to North Korea in bilateral negotiations to convince Pyongyang to give up its current nuclear weapons.

Additionally, the United States should stand up a Country Reconstruction and Stability Group (CRSG) for North Korea right now. Internally, it should treat North Korea as a fragile state, and adopt the social and economic programmatic options in the USAID Fragile States Strategy as agenda items. These broad categories include actions promoting economic growth and management of natural resources, improving revenues generation and expenditures, reforming and building of technical and administrative civil service responsibility for economic management and food security, and ensuring public health and basic education.[89] Planners should look to the Nixon era opening of China as a blueprint, and consider reforms in production, corruption control, legal infrastructure, economic policies, and foreign debt consolidation and relief. The CRSG should study the existing North Korean infrastructure to see if it can support recommendations from the economic portion of this plan.

The group should have representation of all departments of government, including members of Congress, and be headed by the State Department. It should include input from International Non-Governmental Organizations (INGO) on the ground in North Korea now. It should have administration approval and direction, and it should be managed with an incredible amount of personal leadership from the Secretary of State and the President. The economic plan developed should explore nuclear technology that supports energy production but not weapons technology in addition to fuel oil energy solutions currently in place. The plan should also include hard budget figures for implementation, making Congressional participation crucial.

Motivation for such a plan is rooted in strategy as well. The United States National Security Strategy (NSS) discusses the promotion of global economic growth and promotes economic freedom as a means to develop "the free flow of ideas; with increased trade and foreign investment comes exposure to new ways of thinking and living which

---

[89] Andrew Natsios, *Fragile States Strategy* (Washington D.C.: U.S. Agency for International Development, January 2005), 7.

gives citizens more control over their own lives."[90] Planning for the modernization of the North Korean economy as part of an overarching Global War on Terrorism strategy to contain nuclear proliferation and destroy existing nuclear weapons is a prudent development for all people on the Korean peninsula. It also allows the Western world to finally engage what some feel is the true crisis on the peninsula – the ongoing humanitarian crisis that all North Korean have felt under the tyrannical rule of Kim Il Sung and Kim Jong Il.

C. Summary

Opening up a bilateral dialogue with North Korea in support of GWOT objectives will allow the United States to independently pursue nuclear non-proliferation. Success will not hinge on the actions of four other countries that may or may not have the best interests of the United States at hand. Economic aid, normalized relations, and a security guarantee in exchange for the destruction of all nuclear weapons is a small price to pay to be certain that these weapons of mass destruction do not end up in enemy hands. Stopping the proliferation of these weapons through negotiation is much less a price to pay than the cost of having to defend against the use of these weapons in the ongoing Global War on Terrorism.

Of course, there is no certainty that Kim Jong Il will come to terms with the United States on these issues. There is no guarantee that North Korea will even want to adopt any policy developed by the Western world. However, possible failure cannot be a deterrent to good faith negotiations. It is imperative that Washington convince

[90] Bush, 27.

Pyongyang that political, social and economic modernization is a stronger deterrent than nuclear weapons, in turn making nuclear weapon proliferation a less attractive option. In today's strategic environment, using elements of national power other than the military to affect change on the Korean peninsula is a strategic and absolute necessity.

VII. CONCLUSION

Capitalizing on the recent momentum of the successful Six-Party Talks, the United States should begin a line of bilateral negotiations with North Korea outside of the Six-Party Talks. These bilateral negotiations will allow the United States to meet its strategic goals related to the Global War on Terrorism that apply to North Korea, including the elimination of the North Korean nuclear threat.

The current Six-Party Talks agreement, not yet implemented, provides for a discontinuation of North Korea's nuclear program but states nothing on the subject of Pyongyang's current nuclear arsenal. Engaging North Korea on the subjects of economic aid, normalized relations, and a security guarantee will provide strong motivation for Kim Jong Il to destroy his current weapons. Kim Jong Il desires security above all else, both externally and internally. These steps will help him maintain security and alleviate aggression from both the international community and any internal strife caused by economic deficiencies.

The Bush Administration's refusal to negotiate bilaterally for the last six years has done nothing but allow North Korea to develop nuclear weapons and gain a strategic upper hand when dealing with international negotiators trying to come to a negotiated settlement. The Clinton Administration did have a framework in place with North Korea, but the Bush Administration walked away from it after confirming North Korea's clandestine nuclear programs in violation of the agreement. Many say it was inevitable that North Korea would continue with its program, as that is the nature of tyrannical regimes – these regimes need a security threat to validate the prescribed form of government and way of life, and will seek power through any means possible, including international deception and breaking agreements.

Understanding the history of North Korea provides clues to how to negotiate with the regime. North Korea has had little opportunity throughout history for self-determination. From the end of World War II to the collapse of the Soviet Union, North Korea has been only a pawn in a greater game of worldwide chess. Since the end of the Korean War, North Korea has been faced with United States staring it down through the Demilitarized Zone along the 38th parallel, and since the demise of its Soviet backer has tried to develop its own independent means of security. It has surprised no one that nuclear weapons are the result of that perceived security threat. The demand for bilateral negotiations supports Pyongyang's desires to be treated as an equal.

Reviewing the regional interests of those involved in negotiations shows that even nations seemingly united in a cause can have very diverse international and domestic agendas. Throughout the Six-Party Talks, Japan and the United States have publicly maintained a hard line approach to North Korea, in effect not giving in on any issue while waiting for sanctions to reach its inevitable conclusion of regime change. Russia, China, and South Korea all maintained a more realistic approach, and want to engage North Korea across all elements of national power in an effort to provide a motivation strong enough for North Korea to relent in its pursuit of a viable nuclear weapons program.

Understanding that there are two opposing approaches to this equation, relevant case studies must be reviewed to understand a nation's motivation for pursuing weapons of mass destruction, and subsequent motivation for denouncing programs or destroying weapons. Libya and Ukraine are relevant case studies – Libya being the subject of the hard line approach and Ukraine being the subject of the soft line approach. In the end, both countries valued security more than the weapons program itself. Security is more than military security, and in both cases here, it was economic security that was a bigger factor than military security. For South Africa, the only country to destroy an entire arsenal of nuclear weapons, the lack of a military security threat was the prime motivator to do so. These countries provide strong examples of employable methods when negotiating with North Korea.

Government policy should be rooted in objectives and interests but not in emotion. Clearly understanding grand strategy in the context of all elements of national power is essential to proper execution of that policy. The Global War on Terrorism has been promulgated as a generational struggle across all elements of national, regional, and local government. As such, all strategic interests worldwide should be developed to support this overarching grand strategy. Engaging North Korea bilaterally in support of nuclear non-proliferation efforts would be in concert with this effort. Working towards a North Korean security guarantee, normalized relations, and advanced economic aid also addresses the two other key national interests in the region. Deterring a second Korean War and maintaining a strong relationship with the people of the Korean peninsula are likely successful second order effects of bilateral talks with Pyongyang. Bilateral negotiations between Washington and Pyongyang is thus in the best interests of the United States.

BIBLIOGRAPHY

Albright, David Albright. *South Africa's Nuclear Weapons Program.* Institute for Science and International Security, 14 March 2001, accessed 20 January 2007; available at http://web.mit.edu/ssp/seminars/wed_archives_01spring/albright.htm; Internet.

Brookes, Peter. "What Does North Korea Want?" *The Heritage Foundation,* 7 May 2003, accessed 3 October 2006; available from http://www.heritage.org.Press/Commentary/ed050703.cfm; Internet.

Bush, George W. *The National Security Strategy of The United States of America.* Washington, DC: The White House, 2006.

Chen, Jian. *China's Road to the Korean War.* New York: Columbia University Press, 1994.

"Country Profile: North Korea." London: The Economist Intelligence Unit, 2006.

"Country Report: North Korea." London: The Economist Intelligence Unit, August 2006.

Creekmore, Jr., Marion. *A Moment of Crisis: Jimmy Carter, The Power of a Peacemaker, and North Korea's Nuclear Ambitions.* New York: Public Affairs, 2006.

Cummings, Bruce. *Korea's Place in the Sun: A Modern History.* New York: W.W. Norton, 1997.

Denisov, Valery. "Nuclear Crisis on the Korean Peninsula." *International Affairs,* Vol. 50 no. 6 (2004): 47.

"Direct Talks Urged With N. Korea." *The Washington Times*, 23 October 2006.

Elliott, Michael. "The Chinese Century." *Time*, January 22, 2007, 32-42.

Ford, Glyn. *EU Parliamentarian: Six-Party Talks Hostage to Differing Desires.* Honolulu, HI: East-West Center, 2006, accessed 24 October 2006; available from http://www.eastwestcenter.org/events-en-detail.asp?news_ID=353; Internet.

Friedman, Thomas L. *The Lexus and the Olive Tree.* New York: Anchor Books, 2000.

Frontline. *Kim's Nuclear Gamble.* Public Broadcasting System, accessed 15 January 2007, available from http://www.pbs.org/wgbh/pages/frontline/frontline/shows/kim; Internet.

Getz, Arlene. *Q&A: F.W. de Klerk on Iran, Nukes.* Newsweek Web Exclusive, 12 May 2006, accessed 20 January 2007; available at http://www.msnbc.msn.com/id/12758097/site/newsweek; Internet.

Gifford, Rob. *China and Its Neighbors, Part 4, South Korea.* Washington D.C.: National Public Radio, 17 February 2004, accessed 26 November 2006; available from http://www.npr.org/templates/story/story.php?storyId=1680309; Internet.

Hearing before the Subcommittee on Asia and the Pacific of the Committee on International Relations, House of Representatives. "North Korean Nuclear Negotiations: Strategies and Prospects for Success." One Hundred Ninth Congress, Serial No. 109-73, Washington D.C.: Government Printing Office, 14 July 2005.

Hearing before the Committee on Foreign Relations, United States Senate. "U.S. Policy Toward North Korea: Where Do We Go From Here?" One Hundred Seventh Congress, Washington, D.C.: Government Printing Office, 23 May 2001.

Hersh, Seymour M. *Chain of Command.* New York: Harper Collins Publishers, 2004.

Holmes, James R. "Lessons of the Korean War for the Six Party Talks". *World Affairs,* Vol. 169 Iss. 1 (Summer 2006): 3-25.

House of Councilors. *Constitution of Japan.* Tokyo: The National Diet of Japan, accessed 23 October 2006; available from http://www.sangiin.go.jp/eng/law/index.htm; Internet.

Huntley, Wade. "Waiting to Exhale: The Six-Party Talks Agreement." Silver City, NM & Washington D.C.: Foreign Policy in Focus, 25 October 2005.

Joint Publication 1: Joint Warfare of the Armed Forces of the United States. Washington D.C.: Joint Chiefs of Staff, 14 November 2000.

Jung, Monica. "The Nuclear Disarmament of Ukraine 1991-1996." Ph.D. diss., Research Institute of Eastern European Studies, University of Bremen, Germany, 1997-2000.

Kang, David C. "Japan: U.S. Partner or Focused on Abductees?" *The Washington Quarterly,* Vol. 28, no. 4 (Autumn 2005): 107-117.

Kaplan, Fred. "Rolling Blunder: How the Bush Administration let North Korea get Nukes." *Washington Monthly,* May 2004, accessed 13 September 2006; available from http://www.washintonmonthly.com/features/2004/0405.kaplan.html; Internet.

Kim, Taegi, and Kim Hong Kee. "Korea's Bilateral Trade with Japan and the U.S.: A Comparative Study." *Seoul Journal of Economics,* Vol. 12 no. 3 (Fall 1999): 239-57.

Kessler, Glenn. "Conservatives rip N. Korea deal." *The Washington Post,* 14 February 2007, accessed 15 February 2007; available from http://www.msnbc.msn.com/id/17142304; Internet.

The Korean Peninsula Energy Development Organization. *Agreed Framework Between The United States of America and The Democratic People's Republic of Korea.* Geneva, 21 October 1994, Section I.3.

Lam Peng Er. "Japan's Differing Approaches on the Apology Issue to China and South Korea." *American Asian Review (U.S.),* Vol. 20 no. 3 (Autumn 2002): 31-54.

Laney, James T. and Stapleton, Jason T. "How to deal with North Korea." *Foreign Affairs*, Vol. 82 no. 2 (March/April 2003), accessed 13 February 2007; available from http://www.foreignaffairs.org/20030301faessay10336/james-t-laney-jason-t-shaplen/how-to-deal-with-north-korea.html; Internet.

Lee, Forrest. *China Vows to Cut Short Red Tape.* Beijing: People's Daily, 10 January 2003, accessed 26 November 2006; available from http://english.people.com.cn/200301/10/eng20030110_109907.shtml; Internet.

Library of Congress Federal Research Division. *South Korea Country Study.* Washington DC: Library of Congress, 2005, accessed 18 February 2007; available from http://lcweb2.loc.gov/cgi-bin/query/r?frd:@field(DOCID+kr0022); Internet.

"Libya Country Profile." *Nuclear Threat Initiative.* Monterey Institute of International Studies: Center for Nonproliferation Studies, November 2006, accessed 2 January 2007; available from http://www.nti.org/e_research/profiles/Libya.html; Internet.

Lobe, Jim. *Korea Deal Marks Big Victory for Realists.* Inter Press Service News Agency, 14 February 2007, accessed 14 February 2007; available from http://www.ipsnews.net/news.asp?idnews=36552; Internet.

Liu, Melinda. "Can China Play Hardball Diplomacy?" *Newsweek Web Exclusive*, 8 February 2007, accessed 9 February 2007; available from http://www.msnbc.msn.com/id/17051760/site/newsweek/; Internet.

Mann, James. *Rise of the Vulcans.* New York: Penguin Books, 2004

Masaki, Hisane. "Abe's Multiple Policy Dilemmas." *Asian Times,* 28 September 2006, accessed 24 October 2006; available from http://www.atimes.com/atimes/Japan/HI28Dh01.html; Internet.

Masaki, Hisane. "Japan pushes the boundaries of self defense." *Asian Times,* 12 September 2006, accessed 26 October 2006; available from http://www.atimes.com/atimes/Japan/HI12Dh01.html; Internet.

Murdock, Clark A. *Beyond Goldwater-Nichols: Defense Reform for a New Strategic Era.* Washington, DC: Center for Strategic and International Studies, 2004.

Myers, Richard B. *National Military Strategy of the United States of America.* Washington, DC: Joint Chiefs of Staff, 2004.

Natsios, Andrew. *Fragile States Strategy.* Washington D.C.: U.S. Agency for International Development, January 2005.

Niksch, Larry and Perl, Raphael. *North Korea: Terrorism List Removal?* Congressional Research Service report for Congress, 12 August 2004.

"North Korea Country Profile." *Nuclear Threat Initiative.* Monterey Institute of International Studies: Center for Nonproliferation Studies, August 2006, accessed 13 October 2006; available from http://www.nti.org/e_research/profiles/NK/Nuclear/index_157.html; Internet.

"North Korea's Political, Economic Gamble." *The Washington Post,* 10 October 2006, sec. A, p. 12.

Office of Management and Budget. *FY-07 Budget.* Washington, DC: U.S. Government Printing Office, 2006, accessed 20 November 2006; available from http://www.whitehouse.gov/omb/pdf/Economy-07.pdf.; Internet.

Pace, Peter. *National Military Strategic Plan for the War on Terrorism.* Washington DC: Joint Chiefs of Staff, 2006).

Pan, Esther. *North Korea: The Current State of Play.* Council on Foreign Relations, 10 January 2004, accessed on 24 December 2006; available from http://www.cfr.org/publications/7836/north_korea.html; Internet.

Park, John S. "Inside Multilateralism: The Six-Party Talks." *The Washington Quarterly* Vol. 28, no. 4 (Autumn 2005): 75-91.

People's Daily. *The charisma of China's shuttle diplomacy reappears.* Beijing: People's Daily Online, 11 November 2003, accessed 9 January 2007; available from http://english.peopledaily.com.cn/200311/10/eng20031110_127987.shtml; Internet.

Pollack, Jonathan D. "The United States, North Korea, and The End of the Agreed Framework." *Naval War College Review,* Vol. LVI, no. 3 (Summer 2003), accessed 22 February 2007; available from http://www.nwc.navy.mil/press/Review/2003/Summer/art1-su3.htm; Internet.

Quinomes, C. Kenneth. Review of *A Moment of Crisis: Jimmy Carter, The Power of a Peacemaker, and North Korea's Nuclear Ambitions,* by Marion Creekmore, Jr. *Arms Control Association*, (December 2006): accessed 10 January 2007, available from http://www.armscontrol.org/act/2006_12/BookReview.asp; Internet.

Robbins, Carla Anne. "In Giving Up Arms Libya Hopes to Gain New Economic Life." *Wall Street Journal,* 12 February 2004, A1.

Rothschild, Matthew. "Bush at West Point: Vows Long Middle Eastern War, Spreads the Fallacy of the Cold War Analogy." *The Progressive,* 27 May 2006, accessed 10 February 2007; available from http://www.progressive.org/mag_wx052706; Internet.

Rumsfeld, Donald H. *The National Defense Strategy of The United States of America.* Washington, DC: U.S. Government Printing Office, 2005.

Sinai, Joshua. "Libya's Pursuit of Weapons of Mass Destruction." *The Nonproliferation Review,* (Spring-Summer 1997): 92.

"South Africa Country Profile." *Nuclear Threat Initiative.* Monterey Institute of International Studies: Center for Nonproliferation Studies, February 2006, accessed 13 October 2006; available from http://www.nti.org/e_research/profiles/SAfrica/Nuclear/print/index_2153.prt; Internet.

"South Korea Country Profile." *Nuclear Threat Initiative.* Monterey Institute of International Studies: Center for Nonproliferation Studies, August 2006, accessed 13 October 2006; available from http://www.nti.org/e_research/profiles/SKorea/Nuclear/3045_3117.html; Internet.

South Korean Participatory Defense Policy 2003, accessed 27 December 2006; available from http://www.mnd.go.kr/jungchaek/baekseo/2003/2003main_eng.pdf; Internet.

Speech by President George W. Bush, Capitol Hilton Hotel, Washington D.C., 5 September 2006; transcript accessed 10 February 2007; available from http://www.whitehouse.gov/news/releases/2006/09/20060905-4.html; Internet.

Statement of Assistant Secretary for Verification and Compliance Paula A. DeSutter, U.S. Government's Assistance to Libya in the Elimination of its Weapons of Mass Destruction (WMD) before the Senate Foreign Relations Committee, 26 February 2004.

Statement of Secretary of Defense Donald H. Rumsfeld, FY 2007 Posture Statement before The House Armed Services Committee, 8 February 2006.

Stueck, William. *Rethinking The Korean War*. Princeton: Princeton University Press, 2002.

Tam, Kitty. "China's Intervention in the Korean War." *The Brownstone Journal* Vol. VII, no. 1 (Spring 1998): 16-20.

U.S. Defense Department. *Allied Contributions to the Common Defense.* Washington D.C., July 2003, accessed 19 February 2007; available from http://www.defenselink.mil/pubs/allied_contrib2003/allied2003_Chap_1.html; Internet.

U.S. State Department Bureau of East Asian and Pacific Affairs. *Background Note: North Korea.* October 2006 accessed 14 January 2007; available from http://www.state.gov/r/pa/ei/bgn/2792.htm; Internet.

U.S. State Department. *Fifth Round of Six-Party Talks—End of Talks Transit—Traders Hotel.* 11 November 2005 accessed 27 December 2006; available from http://www.state.gov/p/eap/rls/rm/2005/56876.htm; Internet.

U.S. State Department. *Foreign Relations of the United States: Diplomatic Papers: The Conference of Berlin (The Potsdam Conference).* Washington D.C.: U.S. Government Printing Office, 1945, accessed 17 February 2007; available from http://digital.library.wisc.edu/1711.dl/FRUS.FRUS1945Berlinv02; Internet.

U.S. State Department. *Joint Statement of the Fourth Round of the Six-Party Talks.* Washington D.C.: Bureau of Public Affairs, 19 September 2005, accessed 23 October 2006; available from http://www.state.gov/r/pa/prs/ps/2005/53490.htm; Internet.

U.S. State Department. *North Korea Agrees To Abandon Its Nuclear Weapons Programs.* 19 September 2005 accessed 27 December 2006; available from http://usinfo.state.gov/eap/Archive/2005/Sep/19-210095.html; Internet.

"U.S. tables North Korea proposal." *BBC News/Asia Pacific.* London: BBC News, 20 December 2006, accessed 27 December 2006; available from http://news.bbc.co.uk/1/low/world/asia-pacific/6192323.stm; Internet.

"U.S. Vows Not to Be Intimidated by North Korean Threats." Fox News, accessed 23 October 2006; available from http://www.foxnews.com/story/0,2933,219121,00.html; Internet.

"What Does Disarmament Look Like?" The White House, January 2003, accessed 2 January 2007; available from http://www.whitehouse.gov/infocus/iraq/disarmament/disarmament.pdf; Internet.

Woodward, Bob. *Bush At War.* New York: Simon & Shuster, 2002.

Woolf, Amy F. *91144: Nuclear Weapons in the Former Soviet Union: Location, Command, and Control.* Congressional Research Service Reports: Foreign Affairs and National Defense Division, 27 November 1996, accessed 2 January 2007; available from http://www.fas.org/spp/starwars/crs/91-144.htm; Internet.

Wu, Anne. "What China Whispers to North Korea." *The Washington Quarterly,* Vol. 28, no. 2 (Spring 2005): 35-48.

Yun Duk Min. *Japan's Dual Approach Policy toward North Korea: Past, Present, and Future.* Social Service Research Council, July 2005, accessed 13 September 2006; available from http://northkorea.ssrc.org/Yun/pf; Internet.

VITA

COMMANDER RICHARD J. CHEESEMAN, JR. U. S. NAVY

Commander Cheeseman is a native of Carneys Point, New Jersey and a 1989 graduate of The Pennsylvania State University. After being commissioned through the NROTC program, Commander Cheeseman reported to his first tour of duty in USS SAVANNAH (AOR 4) in January 1990, where he served as Boilers Officer, Main Propulsion Assistant, Auxiliaries Officer, and First Lieutenant. In January 1993, he reported to Precommissioning Unit/USS STOUT (DDG 55) where he served as Navigation Officer. Commander Cheeseman's Division Officer shore tour was as a member of CTF-88, where he served as the Surface Operations and Communications Officer from May 1995 to January 1997.

In August 1997, Commander Cheeseman reported to USS NICHOLAS (FFG 47) where he served as Operations Officer, completing a deployment to the Arabian Gulf and Adriatic Sea as part of Operation NOBLE ANVIL/ALLIED FORCE. In August 1999, Commander Cheeseman reported to COMMANDER, DESTROYER SQUADRON EIGHTEEN as the Staff Operations and Plans Officer.

Following his Department Head tours, Commander Cheeseman opted to remain at sea and reported to COMMANDER CARRIER GROUP EIGHT as Flag Secretary in February 2001. He also served as a Battle Watch Captain while deployed to the Arabian Sea embarked in USS THEODORE ROOSEVELT (CVN 71) as part of Operation ENDURING FREEDOM.

Commander Cheeseman completed his Executive Officer assignment in USS MAHAN (DDG 72) from August 2002 to May 2004. In June 2004 he reported for duty as the Officer in Charge of the U.S. Naval Forces Korea Detachment in Chinhae, South Korea, serving there until June 2006. He is currently a full time student in the Joint Advanced Warfighting School at the Joint Forces Staff College.

Commander Cheeseman is slated to become the Commanding Officer of USS BULKELEY (DDG 84) in December 2007.

Commander Cheeseman's awards include the Meritorious Service Medal, Navy Commendation Medal (6), and the Navy Achievement Medal (2), as well as various other unit awards. He is married to the former Barbara Ann Hellwege of Virginia Beach. He and Barbara have three children, Deanna (24), Bradley (20), and Andrew (18), and one grandchild, Julie (3). Commander Cheeseman is an avid golfer and a big sports fan, and enjoys reading in his spare time.

www.ingramcontent.com/pod-product-compliance
Lightning Source LLC
Chambersburg PA
CBHW081329310526
45789CB00018B/2600
* 9 7 8 1 5 0 0 5 2 0 6 2 5 *